Transforming Family Trauma

Your Essential Guide to Lifelong Recovery
From Adverse Childhood Experiences
and Their Adult Aftermath

Lane Lasater, Ph.D.

Images for Recovery drawn by Janet E. Gustafson

FundamentalLivingSolutions.com

**Practical and Detailed Guides For
Mastering Family & Relationship Challenges
from Dr. Lane Lasater**

Library of Congress Cataloging-in-Publication Data

Lasater, Lane

Transforming Family Trauma: Your Essential Guide to Lifelong Recovery from Adverse Childhood Experiences and Adult Aftermath

Copyright © 2021 FundamentalLivingSolutions.com

First Edition

ISBN: 978-1-7375275-0-3

Trigger and Content Warning: Please be aware that the book includes descriptions of trauma, PTSD, child abuse, alcoholism, family violence, drug addiction, sexual addiction, compulsive behavior patterns including overeating, bulimia, sexual abuse, depression, disability, divorce, anger, sex, and terminal illness which could disturb or trigger upsetting memories for certain readers.

Disclaimer

This book is designed to give you information to help you be successful in your recovery from family trauma during childhood or adulthood if you desire to do so. The information and suggestions provided are for the reader's education and consideration only. Providing information and practical strategies to you about recovery does not constitute the practice of psychotherapy or medicine, and the publisher and author have taken care to alert you to serious warning signs and encourage you to seek licensed professional help when indicated.

The information provided in this book is not a substitute for assessment, diagnosis and treatment of any mental disorder and cannot substitute for the services of a mental health care professional or physician. It is intended for instructional purposes only. The use of this information is solely at your own risk.

The author, seller, partners, and affiliates of this book shall have no liability for claims by, or damages of any kind to, a user of this information. Such damages include, without limitation, damages for personal injuries, emotional distress, and other non-monetary loss, as well as direct or indirect damages. We have made all reasonable efforts to include accurate and up-to-date information to you but make no warranties or representations as to its accuracy, completeness, or timeliness.

Professional Reviews

"It was a joy to read Dr. Lasater's book, *Transforming Family Trauma*. I found it easy reading, engaging, and rich in practical resources. Dr. Lasater's earlier book, *Recovery from Compulsive Behavior*, was useful to me in my practice as a clinical psychologist. This book is intended to help persons working to overcome negative effects of adverse experiences in their childhood family (ACEs), and for healthcare providers who help them. The author's quality of character comes through in his empathy, kindness, and respect for the hurt and dignity of persons who grew up in troubled families. Written in ordinary language, concepts, principles, and exercises are easy to understand and use in recovery from ACEs.

Stages and steps of recovery are clearly outlined and illustrated with real-life stories of people in recovery from hurtful childhood family experiences. There are self-assessments that facilitate self-examination and can remove confusion and show people what sense their current adult lives and struggles make in view of their past family lives. Guidance based on research and clinical experience is offered for healing and transformative change in unstable self-concept, self-defeating thinking and emotional behaviors, troubled relationships, and addictions. Potentially healing "touches" can be felt in some of the descriptions and statements. The book and workbook are replete with resources that support healing, recovery, and maintenance of healthy transformative change."

Reginaldo G. Garcia, Ph.D.
Clinical Psychologist - Alabama & Colorado
Chair, Steering Committee
Farley Health Policy Center, Univ. of Colorado Denver

"Reading *Transforming Family Trauma* is like having a conversation with an old friend, someone you trust, who is on your side and who truly understands you. Fundamental to this book is the respect and regard Dr. Lasater conveys for the person recovering from childhood trauma, for the process of recovery, and the need for support, encouragement, and guidance from a trusted source.

Dr. Lasater's deeply personal account of overcoming family trauma lends credibility to his understanding of damage caused by childhood trauma, the arduous process of overcoming that damage, and the value of resources essential to arriving at the ultimate goal of recovery. With the knowledge, guidance and encouragement described in this book, Dr. Lasater helps you to design your own recovery program for living the life you want to live."

Sonja B. Holt, Ph.D.
Clinical Psychologist, Arvada, Colorado
Adjunct Professor
Psy.D. Training Program
University of Denver

"At last! Dr. Lane Lasater's book will shift your consciousness from just existing as a survivor of the past to a person who is empowered and happier. His comprehensive recovery program is practical and amazingly forceful in sharing a path to emotional freedom. You will be inspired by his coaching because it is based on reclaiming lost joy, love, and compassion. Use it well!"

Ricardo Esparza, Ph.D.
Clinical Psychologist
Boulder, Colorado

Table of Contents

1. Are Childhood Experiences Holding You Back?

"Your wounding, the breaching of your soul, is an invitation to your renaissance."

Jean Huston

Are you still suffering from childhood traumatic events? This book can guide you step-by-step as you move beyond the harmful experiences you faced and overcome their powerful and enduring effects in your adult life. I've walked every step of this path as I healed from my troubled childhood and found my way to wholeness.

Growing up in troubled families, we didn't have the information, support, and resources to comprehend or escape what was happening, and this powerlessness magnified the destructive impact of sometimes catastrophic family events. This book describes how wounded parents and family systems get off track, how traumatic childhood family events continue to harm us, and how to chart your path to self-understanding, well-being, and fulfillment.

As adults, we unintentionally bring with us the desperate strategies we developed as children to survive in our troubled families, and these behaviors often subtly dominate our adult choices. As a result, we walk through our lives carrying invisible wounds, trapped in behavior choices and emotional patterns we feel unable to change. Many of us don't respect ourselves, struggle with depression, anxiety, or anger, and feel lost trying to create healthy relationships and meet adult tasks and challenges. Surrounded by potential addictions, we may turn to alcohol, drugs, cigarettes, food, gambling, sexual affairs, or other escapes to soften the edge of suffering.

Why do so many families offer some life necessities but fail at providing the emotional support, safety and stability children need? Multi-generational transmission of trauma and chaos happens when parents, still struggling with their own childhood wounds, create families, and unwittingly bring with them their ineffective coping patterns, unfinished emotional business, and addictions, and plant these painful seeds in their children.

Through major advances in understanding family systems, the multiple consequences of traumatic experiences, child development, and the dynamics of addictions, we now understand the dangerous and enduring impact troubled family systems can have for those of us who grew up in such environments. Thankfully, the transformative information and resources of *recovery* can empower us to transform our often desperate childhood survival behavior into freedom and serenity.

> Recovery means restoring ourselves to physical, emotional, and spiritual wholeness, or for many of us, reaching a state of health, peace, and life satisfaction we've never experienced or thought possible.

Recovery doesn't mean good as new. We always carry the scars and memories of past painful and negative experiences, but with healing information and support, these adverse events no longer must dominate our emotions and relationships. We can develop ways of living that meet our deepest needs, respect our limitations and vulnerabilities, and open our hearts to love, happiness and gratitude.

The gift of recovery from my traumatic family experiences is the foundation for everything I treasure in life. Recovery principles guide my relationship with my life partner and inspire our family goals. My life's work as a clinical psychologist has focused on supporting other people wounded in their troubled families. My aim in this book is to offer you a complete guide to recovery, and to help you connect you with information and resources that enable you to transform your childhood wounds into strength and wisdom.

The Impact of Family Trauma

The American Psychological Association defines trauma as:

> "Any disturbing experience that results in significant fear, helplessness, dissociation, confusion, or other disruptive feelings intense enough to have a long-lasting negative effect on a person's attitudes, behavior, and other aspects of functioning."

Traumatic experiences we faced as children often overwhelmed our ability to cope with and integrate the powerful emotions that resulted. Such experiences impact our neurological, social, emotional and relationship development. As you know, the adverse events we faced in troubled families often go far beyond what happens in less challenged families. These adverse childhood experiences can devastate us, and may include witnessing family violence, being physically and/or sexually abused by adults, facing abandonment or betrayal, harsh and repeated criticism, a parent who favored another sibling or who couldn't acknowledge your worth, or losing a parent to addiction, divorce, or death.

You may feel intense sadness or resentment when you think about your family experiences, or you may feel numb and dead inside. Whether a specific negative experience is traumatic or deeply painful for you depends on your perspective. Your brother or sister may have shrugged off a certain event, but you felt devastated, yet another experience may have deeply disturbed them, but not you. As we recover, we gradually understand and share our challenging childhood experiences with safe people, recognize and integrate the powerful emotions that remain, and move forward, no longer oppressed by these memories.

Each of us received a unique set of strengths and limitations during childhood. The resources we received in our families and communities helped offset the limitations and catastrophes we may have faced, but many of us still weren't fully prepared for adulthood. Our skill deficits, survival behavior strategies and emotional defenses lead us directly into adult relationship problems, challenging emotions, faulty coping strategies and addictions. These complex adult emotional and behavioral challenges represent an accumulation of choices we made one by one, choices that seemed right at the time but didn't work out the way we hoped. Recovery gives us access to the information and support to face these challenges, empowered with the complete set of resources and skills we need.

How Do We Recover?

With the revolutionary information and resources now widely available, we can understand our childhood strategies with compassion, interrupt and transform self-sabotaging behavior patterns, stop addictions, heal from the hurts of the past, and find new, constructive ways of living. Over time, we can transform our troubled family experience into strength, reduce chronic distress, and devote ourselves to rewarding pursuits and service. Millions of people, just like you, have transformed their troubled childhood experiences, and through the process have become wiser and more effective human beings.

The journey from our childhood traumatic experiences and adult self-defeating behavior to emotional and behavioral freedom is complicated, and most of us can't do it alone. We need experienced helpers, and we need to prepare, plan, study, train, and persevere. There will be more twists and turns than we expect, but we can learn to protect and care for ourselves so childhood experiences and limitations no longer constrain our lives.

As we recover, we gradually change our attitudes and behavior and understand how we often unwittingly perpetuate childhood patterns. A clear understanding of our behavior enables us to develop specific plans to overcome each recovery challenge we face. Here's what this book offers you:

A detailed description of children's adaptive survival emotional and behavior patterns in troubled families.

Exercises and diagnostic self-tests to help you identify which behavior patterns affect you and how they work.

Step-by-step instructions and skills to assist you in moving from self-sabotaging behavior to emotional and behavioral freedom.

Descriptions of the lives of people recovering from these patterns, and

Recovery images to accompany central ideas in this book.

Throughout the book, I use ordinary language descriptions rather than psychological diagnostic terminology (except for PTSD) to describe people's recovery experiences. Psychiatric and Psychological Diagnoses were developed to be a helpful shorthand for professional communication, but the unintentional result is that some people feel dehumanized and disempowered by such labels. The essence of recovery for me is embracing our shared humanity, and through informed individual choices, making the best of our lives no matter what challenges we encounter.

Family Trauma Syndrome

I use the term "family trauma syndrome" to describe three types of problems many adults from troubled families face: *enduring emotional adjustments, self-defeating life patterns,* and *chemical and behavioral addictions.*

1. Enduring Emotional Adjustments

Enduring emotional adjustments began as we adapted to childhood environments where we had few behavior options and couldn't escape. We naturally bring these coping strategies with us into adulthood, long after the need for them—survival—exists. Thus, we unintentionally re-create the limitations of our childhood environments. Here are common enduring emotional adjustments for adults from troubled families:

Unstable self-worth

Unresolved emotions, Post Traumatic Stress Disorder (PTSD), and complex PTSD (C-PTSD—from chronic stress exposure)

Difficulty trusting ourselves and others

2. Self-Defeating Life Patterns

We naturally carry forward as adults the childhood family survival roles we played, and these behaviors frequently become self-defeating life patterns which are difficult to recognize and change, even when they no longer serve our best interests. The following behavior patterns are widespread among those of us who grew up in troubled and traumatic families.

Compulsive Achievement—we're always striving for the next victory or success, often at the expense of health, relationships, and well-being.

Co-Dependency—we repeatedly invest time, energy, and affection in people who don't (or can't) reciprocate what we offer, and neglect our own needs.

Generalized Rebellion—we chronically struggle with and attempt to reform organizations or dysfunctional systems and make ourselves scapegoats.

Casualty Syndrome—we enter unhealthy relationships or job situations naively or passively, and inadvertently set ourselves up to be manipulated, disappointed, victimized, or abandoned.

Under-Responsibility Pattern—we learn to manipulate or charm our way through life, not following through on commitments or fully meeting adult responsibilities.

7

3. Chemical and Behavioral Addictions

Because enduring emotional adjustments and self-defeating life patterns create additional pain and problems for us, we're quite vulnerable to developing chemical or behavioral addictions, including:

- alcohol, drug, and cigarette addiction

- food addiction, including bingeing, self-starvation, and bulimia

- sexual addictions such as pornography, illicit affairs, or hiring sex workers

- compulsive spending

- gambling addiction

Daniel's Behavior Crisis

Daniel's life illustrates how one person overcame unstable self-worth, unresolved emotions, co-dependency, and food addiction during recovery.

Daniel trembled visibly as he recalled a confrontation with his 13-year-old son, Ryan, the night before. "Ryan came home very late, and when I confronted him, he swore at me. I lost it and almost slugged him." The intensity of his anger toward Ryan shocked Daniel. He wanted to get his rage under control before he created a catastrophe.

The Roots of Daniel's Behavior

As Daniel grew up, his parents constantly argued about his father's compulsive achievement. Daniel felt lonely and unaccepted by his father, who traveled for work. He tried to counsel his parents to improve the situation, but his efforts to help failed. Then, when Daniel was a teenager, his mother passed away from a heart attack, and he had to take a lot of responsibility for his younger brothers. He arrived at adulthood feeling unwanted, unworthy, and lonely, and comforted himself with food. His bingeing on high fat, high sugar junk food became an addiction, and now he was quite overweight.

Daniel's co-dependency led him to marry a woman who was irresponsible and not prepared for the commitment of marriage and raising Ryan. As in childhood, Daniel took most of the responsibility in the family, and when his wife abandoned the family, Daniel was alone with responsibility for Ryan.

After the divorce, Daniel devoted himself to taking care of Ryan. He wanted to give Ryan everything he'd missed during his own childhood, but when his son rebelled, it threatened Daniel's unconscious wish to have his son validate him. Daniel tried to control Ryan, but this only hardened this teenager's normal quest for autonomy.

Daniel's Recovery Tasks

Ryan's rebellion forced Daniel to let his son take more responsibility for his choices and become more independent. But facing his son's emancipation triggered Daniel's unacknowledged grief from losing his mother as a teenager and other painful childhood events. As he recognized and shared his childhood pain in therapy, Daniel gradually let go of over-controlling Ryan, who rebelled less intensely. As part of Daniel's self-care, he joined the (OA) Overeaters Anonymous. This gave Daniel a spiritual support system and black and white eating plan that excluded his addictive foods. Over the next few months, Daniel lost 50 pounds and for the first time in his life, felt hopeful about the future and his ability to make positive choices.

The Stages of Behavior Change

We now understand clearly the process of how to change behavior patterns. Prochaska and DiClemente first described this while studying cigarette smokers trying to quit (https://bit.ly/3qXmBQ3). Understanding exactly how people change empowers us, and each step we make toward change becomes a waypoint on the journey toward our recovery goals. This book can lead you through each stage of change as you understand and replace archaic emotional and behavior patterns that no longer work for you.

Recognition happens when you see that a problem or set of problems applies to you.

Hope develops when you learn how other people have overcome similar problems.

Clarity occurs as you comprehend exactly how your problems developed and how they continue.

Decision is your firm commitment to take the actions necessary to overcome these challenges.

Preparation involves gathering the resources and support you need to face the losses, confusion, and uncertainty required for growth and change.

Action takes place over a long period and in small increments as you self-consciously stop old behavior and practice new patterns of action.

Maintenance requires managing your life to support your new self-affirming lifestyle and choices and not creating additional problems.

Chapters 2, 3, 4, 5, 6, 7 and 8 cover the first three stages of behavior change—Recognition, Hope and Clarity.

Chapter 2 tells you my recovery story.

Chapter 3 explains how the strengths and stresses of our childhood environments provide the foundations for both helpful and unhelpful adult behavior patterns.

Chapter 4 describes the ingenious ways we adapted as children to traumatic and adverse experiences and limitations in our families.

Chapters 5, 6, 7 and 8 describe exactly how adult enduring emotional adjustments, self-defeating life patterns, and addictions develop.

Chapters 9 and 10 describe the many recovery resources now available, help you develop your recovery plan, and focus on your decision and preparation steps for recovery.

Chapters 11, 12, 13, 14 and 15 present tools for recovery actions and maintenance of the growth we have achieved.

Image 1 portrays our dilemma as we undertake recovery.

Hitting the Rapids: This canoe on the verge of sinking in raging rapids represents childhood survival strategies that no longer serve us in adulthood. At one time these strategies helped us cope with difficult childhood circumstances, but they no longer work. The negative consequences of enduring emotional adjustments, self-defeating life patterns, and addictions have now become a torrent. The life ring represents recovery information and support from others, which we need to overcome these powerful patterns. To reach the ring, we must abandon the waning security of the canoe and leap to the life ring. This means coming to terms with painful reality and facing powerful emotions. But through the leap, we can receive the help of others and reach the shore.

How to Use this Book

Always respect your personal learning style, but here are specific suggestions on to get the most out of it.

Get the big picture. Read through the entire book to get an overview of the process and steps for moving beyond family trauma and adverse experiences. It's helpful to know the lay of the land when you get into unfamiliar territory.

Keep a recovery journal. Record your work for each exercise as you go through the book. This provides a record of what you've learned and lets you see the progress you're making.

Share your work with someone you trust. When you're ready, tell someone you feel safe with that you're working through the book. You might ask them to complete some exercises for comparison. If you don't have anyone you feel comfortable discussing your exercises with, consider finding a therapist to get the benefit of more support and dialogue.

Keep at it. A short-term approach won't work. There's no quick and easy way to recover—just do your homework. But each step you take counts and your work day-by-day moves you forward steadily on your path to happiness and freedom.

Key Takeaways in this Chapter

- Troubled family systems expose us to great stress, but as children we couldn't protect ourselves and accordingly developed survival behavior adaptations and emotional defenses that frequently become lasting habits.

- Many of us who experienced adverse and traumatic childhood experiences arrive at adulthood with enduring emotional adjustments and self-defeating life patterns that hamper our lives and put us at increased risk for addictions.

- Clearly understanding the dynamics and impact of troubled families helps guide your path to recovery.

- Following the steps of behavior change gives you a map to follow you as you complete the process of transforming your life.

- Millions of people, just like you, have moved beyond childhood trauma and adverse childhood events to create meaningful and fulfilling lives and relationships.

Good luck on your journey!

2. My Journey to Recovery

"Deep inside us, we know what every family therapist knows· the problems between the parents become the problems within the children."

Roger Gould

A Wounded Person

I grew up in rural Colorado, where my parents were cattle ranchers. My childhood family was a powerful blend of my parents who were very caring but also quite wounded, terrible family conflict, wonderful animals and natural beauty, loneliness, joy, and deep hurt. I realized much later that I became a helper as a little boy as I tried to stop my parent's terrible arguments.

When I couldn't make things better, I became angry and rebelled, and our bitter fights tried them greatly. I also turned my anger against myself. By the time I reached drinking age, I was lonely, depressed and alienated and hated myself without really understanding why. I blacked out the first time I drank beer at age 18, and many times thereafter, and for fourteen years, I worked hard to keep my drinking separate from my work and studies.

Discovering My Calling

Fortuitously, after college, I worked for two years in a psychiatric hospital as an attendant where I discovered and fell in love with the world of psychology, which was entirely new to me. This powerful experience led to the decision to become a clinical psychologist, and for the next eight years I worked in hospitals, prisons, and community mental health centers while I completed my professional training at the University of Colorado. My clinical psychology internship at the University of Minnesota Health Sciences Center in Minneapolis was the next step toward fulfilling this dream.

Throughout my professional work and training, I discovered how fascinating it was to understand each stage of people's lives. I observed how each person's development was shaped throughout his or her unique circumstances. It thrilled me to be in this field. The last clinical rotation of my internship was working at a community mental health center in central Minnesota. A few weeks later I would start a one-year fellowship in child, adolescent, and family psychology in Minneapolis. Then, when I finished my doctoral dissertation, my graduate training would be complete. I respected this group of mental health professionals who worked with troubled families coping with alcoholism, child abuse, and violence. During my summer at their clinic, they modeled how to be genuine and loving with the people they served. Their personal wisdom, developed from broad life experiences, gave them deep compassion for people and families in pain. I wanted to be that kind of helper.

A Painful Awakening

Before we finished our time at the mental health center, the staff held a goodbye party for me and my fellow psychology intern. After volleyball and a cookout, we sat drinking wine and talking, enjoying the cool summer evening. I kept drinking wine as the evening went on. We talked about our families, and trying to be funny, I talked about a time at age eleven when I tried unsuccessfully to stop my parents' violent argument. I laughed about my ineffectiveness as a family therapist. My friends greeted my story with silence. I instantly regretted opening my mouth because I'd revealed my troubled family background, and that I was emotionally unfinished with the past.

For a long time, I'd kept secret my shame about my troubled childhood because I feared it made me emotionally unworthy to become a psychologist. Until that moment, I'd considered my professional training almost complete. Over the next few months, it became apparent that the last and most important dimension of my preparation as a helper was only starting. I had to make peace with my troubled childhood experiences.

During the weeks after the party, I struggled to come to terms with my feelings about the past. I recognized I needed professional help and asked my clinical supervisor at the University to recommend a therapist. She recommended clinical social worker Merle Fossum (<u>Facing Shame: Families in Recovery</u>) in Saint Paul.

Discovering Recovery

At our first meeting, Merle asked me many questions about my family life growing up. He was also interested in my drinking. During the second session, Merle told me he thought I was in trouble with alcohol, and recommended that

I stop drinking. Even though I knew he was right, my heart sank. Drinking gave me breaks from life and seemed to help me cope with my emotions and relationships. With Merle's help, I realized I'd been an alcoholic from my earliest drinking experiences. I thought the purpose of drinking was to get drunk. I'd struggled for years to drink in a controlled way. Now the secret was out.

I haven't had a drink since that day. Merle introduced me to people who showed how to create a fulfilling life without drinking. As I removed the anesthetic of alcohol, my emotions awakened. I didn't realize it then, but I had miles to go in recovery. After I'd stopped drinking for a few months, Merle recommended I complete an outpatient treatment program for alcoholics and their families. He told me I needed to face my traumatic childhood experiences so I could maintain recovery. The powerful treatment program I entered in Minneapolis, developed by Dr. Patrick Carnes (A Gentle Path through the Twelve Steps), helped me heal the anger, hurt, and shame from childhood.

Deeper Healing

An important milestone in recovery came after I'd stopped drinking for several years. I heard Dr. Claudia Black speak in Colorado Springs about adult children of from alcoholic families (It Will Never Happen to Me: Children of Alcoholics as Youngsters—Adolescents—Adults). Dr. Black's moving talk touched me profoundly, and initially I felt shattered as a flood of grief came over me. Many painful memories returned, and I recognized how deeply traumatic some family experiences were for my siblings and me. My grieving continued for months, but finally a lightness and peace I'd never felt before gradually came over me.

As my sadness about my family ebbed, I felt great compassion for my wounded parents, who did everything they could to give us a good start in life. I recognized that what happened in my family resulted from several generations of unfinished emotional business and troubled family patterns. Even though my parents sought help, the professionals they saw didn't have the information and resources to intervene in this destructive family cycle. I deeply regret my parent's suffering, but treasure the wisdom and kindness they shared with me and my siblings, which benefits me every day.

Grateful for the Life I've Been Given

Amid the conflict, hurt and trauma in my family, there were many resources as well. The entire family worked together each summer. My father taught my brothers, my sister, and me how to ride horses and raise and care for our animals and to respect nature and the environment. My mother loved people and showed great kindness to everyone she met. She showed me how to take care of others, and this inspired me in my work as a psychologist. My parents believed in education and helped with mine. Their values uplifted me through the years as I worked to help other people make the best of their lives.

In recovery, I had to give up trying to change the organizations where I worked, and stop expecting my family members to change. I had to stop smoking cigarettes, stop my sugar addiction and compulsive achieving, and learn to care for my health. The negative events in my life ceased to dominate me emotionally. I learned to appreciate my life as it was, realizing I became a more compassionate and helpful person because I understand recovery struggles firsthand. Through my recovery and professional experience, and the kindness and support of so many people, I now understand how to transform troubled behavior and emotional patterns into strength and wisdom. Through this book I share my knowledge about wounded children and families, self-help resources, and therapy, bodywork and meditation tools that have all been part of my process to support you on your recovery journey.

Key takeaways from this chapter

- During recovery, I've learned to solve my problems one at a time, taking on the most pressing issues first.
- Alcohol was my primary escape, but I had to stop cigarettes, and sugar, wheat, flour, and high-fat foods as well.
- Self-help group support, addiction treatment, trauma therapy, bodywork and meditation are resources for many people during recovery.
- Numbed or frozen feelings slowly un-thaw during recovery, and it can take several years to process these emotions and come to peace with the past.
- You have the ultimate power to change your life using compassionate language for yourself and the wealth of resources available.

3. Childhood Challenges and Childhood Resources

"It is impossible for a mother or father to avoid passing something of their own traumatic experiences on to their children through the process of bonding. These are the deeper feelings, perceptions, thoughts and embodied ways of being which form the residue of the trauma."

Franz Ruppert

Why do so many of us face family trauma and other adverse experiences during childhood? We now know that family troubles pass from generation to generation when children adapt to the limitations of their parents, and then as adults unknowingly convey these limitations to their own children. As we reach adulthood, we strive to emancipate from our families and attain behavioral and emotional freedom from our childhood limitations. We often find it's more difficult to separate than we realized, but now we can access the resources and information we need to interrupt these multigenerational patterns of family troubles and addiction.

How do our childhood environments lead to adult emotional and behavioral problems? How do we evaluate difficult childhood experiences? This chapter helps you understand both the challenges you faced and the resources you received from your childhood family and community. The resources we received helped offset the impact of adverse experiences and trauma, but unfortunately, for many of us, our challenges outweighed our resources. So, we must work hard during recovery to gain additional information and learn new skills to bring ourselves into balance as functioning adults.

Because our family is our first learning context, it serves as the template for adult behavior. We watch our parents and model their behavior, and learn directly and indirectly from our families about relationships, how to view the world, and how to behave. We receive (often unconscious) powerful constructive and destructive messages from parenting figures such as "I love you," "You're a good girl," "It's okay to make mistakes," "I'm glad you're here," "Get a good education," or "You're stupid," "You don't belong here," "That's not good enough," "Don't bother me," "Don't expect too much," and "You're a mistake."

Siblings often experience quite different family environments because of changes in family finances or parents' relationship, the progression of addictions, the departure of older siblings, and whether grandparents or other relatives are available to us. We rarely knew too much about other families, so we assumed our family was representative. If problems predominated over family strengths, we instinctively learned that our goal was to survive.

The more we understood ourselves and developed emotional and relationship skills, the more choices we had and the more enhanced our lives became, or vice versa. Coping with our troubled families frequently required us to over-learn certain skills while not learning others, so we become adept at the skills we practiced frequently. Our pattern of skills and deficits then prepared us either well or poorly to cope with adult responsibilities and challenges.

Your family may have provided an environment rich in emotional expression, yet lacking in encouragement for intellectual curiosity and development. You may have found it necessary to take responsibility beyond your years, but because of an unsupportive emotional environment and your lack of preparation, these responsibilities were overwhelming and filled you with fear. You may have learned that adults relax and have fun by drinking alcohol, or that playing games and working on hobbies is fun, or that adults never relax because they're always working.

Now you have the power, information, support, and resources to identify and correct the emotional and skill imbalances you experienced. During recovery you recognize and replace beliefs, skills and survival strategies that don't serve your best interests. This book leads you through the process of evaluating your child and teenage experiences so you can effectively remediate their adult aftermath.

Adverse Childhood Events (ACEs)

Drs. Vincent J. Felitti and Robert F. Anda and colleagues conducted breakthrough research in 1998 titled "The Adverse Childhood Experiences Study" (bit.ly/3hE8n24) that showed a significant correlation between adverse childhood events and many of the leading causes of death in adults.

They studied a sample of 9,508 men and women (all who had health insurance coverage through Kaiser in San Diego).

Participants first received a standardized medical evaluation which assessed adult risk behavior, overall health status and disease, and then completed a mail survey which asked them about seven categories of adverse childhood experiences: psychological, physical, or sexual abuse; violence against mother; or living with household members who were substance abusers, mentally ill or suicidal; or ever imprisoned.

Recovery Exercise #1: Complete the ACEs questionnaire below.

Prior to your 18th Birthday	Yes	No
1. Did a parent or other adult in the household often or very often... Swear at you, insult you, put you down, or humiliate you? or Act in a way that made you afraid that you might be physically hurt?		
2. Did a parent or other adult in the household often or very often... Push, grab, slap, or throw something at you? or Ever hit you so hard that you had marks or were injured?		
3. Did an adult or person at least 5 years older than you ever... Touch or fondle you or have you touch their body in a sexual way? or Attempt or actually have oral, anal, or vaginal intercourse with you?		
4. Did you often or very often feel that ... No one in your family loved you or thought you were important or special? or Your family didn't look out for each other, feel close to each other, or support each other?		
5. Did you often or very often feel that ... You didn't have enough to eat, had to wear dirty clothes, and had no one to protect you? or Your parents were too drunk or high to take care of you or take you to the doctor if you needed it?		
6. Were your parents ever separated or divorced?		
7. Was your mother or stepmother: Often or very often pushed, grabbed, slapped, or had something thrown at her? or Sometimes, often, or very often kicked, bitten, hit with a fist, or hit with something hard? or Ever repeatedly hit over at least a few minutes or threatened with a gun or knife?		
7. Did you live with anyone who was a problem drinker or alcoholic, or who used street drugs?		
8. Was a household member depressed or mentally ill, or did a household member attempt suicide?		
9. Did a household member go to prison?		
Total your "Yes" answers for your ACEs score.		

Understanding Your ACEs Score

Your total possible score is 10. Two-thirds of their respondents reported a score of one, and 87% reported a score of two or more. **In their findings, a score of four or more adverse childhood experiences was associated with increased risk of disease, social and health problems.** Below are the percentage breakdowns for scores of zero to three, and four or more ACEs.

Number of Adverse Childhood Experiences (ACE Score)	Women %	Men %	Total %
0	34.5	38.0	36.1
1	24.5	27.9	26.0
2	15.5	16.4	15.9
3	10.3	8.6	9.5
4 or more	15.2	9.2	12.5

Here's their summary of the relationship between ACEs scores and health risk behavior and diseases.

"More than half of respondents reported at least one, and one-fourth reported ≥ 2 categories of childhood exposures. We found a graded relationship between the number of categories of childhood exposure and each of the adult health risk behaviors and diseases that were studied (P <.001). Persons who had experienced four or more categories of childhood exposure, compared to those who had experienced none, had 4- to 12-fold increased health risks for alcoholism, drug abuse, depression, and suicide attempt; a 2- to 4-fold increase in smoking, poor self-rated health, ≥ 50 sexual intercourse partners, and sexually transmitted disease; and a 1.4- to 1.6- fold increase in physical inactivity and severe obesity. The number of categories of adverse childhood exposures showed a graded relationship to future adult diseases including ischemic heart disease, cancer, chronic lung disease, skeletal fractures, and liver disease. The seven categories of adverse childhood experiences were strongly interrelated, and persons with multiple categories of childhood exposure were likely to have multiple health risk factors later in life."

Your ACEs Score

My Adverse Childhood Experiences score was six. This confirmed what I already knew—I'm a very high-risk person and my recovery from ACEs, family trauma and addiction is a life and death matter for me. Whatever your risk score is, please know that every action you take toward recovery counts. Your recovery efforts are deadly serious.

Resilience Resources for Youth

The National Health Service of Wales in 2018 conducted a major study of family and community conditions in that country to assess the extent to which resilience resources available to youth offset the long-term risks for youth with high ACEs scores (bit.ly/3xhEfAa). They asked adults to complete retrospectively the Child and Youth Resilience Measure (CYR-M) and compared scores with participants' health data.

Recovery Exercise #2: Complete the Child and Youth Resilience Questionnaire.

Complete that questionnaire below to assess resilience resources available to you as a child that may have helped you offset effects of ACEs and family traumatic experiences.

When you were growing up, during the first 18 years of life, to what extent would the following sentences have described you? Place an X below the box that best describes how true this statement was for you.	Not at all	A Little	Some what	Quite a bit	A Lot
1. I had people I looked up to.					
2. Getting an education was important to me.					
3. My parents/caregivers knew a lot about me.					
4. I tried to finish activities that I started.					
5. I was able to solve problems without harming myself or others (e.g. without using drugs or being violent.)					
6. I knew where to go in my community to get help.					
7. I felt I belonged in my school.					
8. My family would stand by me during difficult times.					
9. My friends would stand by me during difficult times.					
10. I was treated fairly in my community.					
11. I had opportunities to develop skills to help me succeed in life (like job skills and skills to care for others).					
12. I enjoyed my community's cultures and traditions.					
Note the total number of Xs you marked in the columns titled "Quite a bit" and "A Lot." This total number is your resilience resource score.					

Resilience Resources Findings of the Welsh Study

The researchers grouped participants into three levels of childhood resilience. (a) **Low childhood resilience** <6 positive items (10.9% of participants); (b) **Moderate**

childhood resilience 6-9 positive items (19.4% of participants); and (c) **High childhood** resilience 10-12 positive items (69.7% of participants). The authors found that resilience resources did somewhat lower the risks of mental illness both in those who report ACEs and those who do not.

- In multivariate analyses (including socio-demographics, ACE count and childhood resilience category), higher ACE count remained strongly associated with increased risk of all mental illness categories, and higher childhood resilience with reduced risk (p<0.001).

- Individuals who suffered ACEs were at significantly increased risk of mental illness, with risks of all outcomes increasing with the number of ACEs reported. Compared with people with no ACEs, those reporting four or more were over three times more likely to report current mental illness, six times more likely to report lifetime mental illness and nine times more likely to report having ever felt suicidal or self-harmed.

- Individuals who suffered ACEs had fewer resilience resources, with markers of both childhood and adulthood resilience reducing as ACE counts increased (see Sections 4 and 5). Thus, those with four or more ACEs had the lowest exposure to individual, relationship and community factors that may build resilience.

- Both childhood and adult resilience resources showed protective relationships with mental illness independent of ACEs. Thus, resilience resources may lower the risks of mental illness both in those who report ACEs and those who do not. However, resilience does not provide a panacea to ACEs, and primary prevention of ACEs must remain a key priority.

Your Resilience Resources Score

Your score on this scale helps you take stock of the resources that were available to you. Also note the resources that you didn't have and try to make those a priority for you during recovery. The higher your resilience resources score, the better.

My resilience resources score was seven, which they classify as moderate as you saw above. My parents tried very hard to do their best for us but couldn't overcome their conflicts because the professionals they sought help from didn't understand alcoholism and family dynamics and weren't able to help. Further, because we lived in a rural area, I had minimal contact with other families and community resources. I did okay in school, which helped me get by even though my emotional problems prevented me from retaining what I learned until much later when I discovered psychology and pursued a field that deeply interested me.

Basic Human Needs

Another useful way to understand how we coped with our childhood environments is our ability to meet basic human needs, a concept introduced by Abraham Maslow (<u>Motivation and Personality</u>). When we can't fulfill our basic human needs, we're at greater risk of developing enduring emotional adjustments, self-defeating life patterns and addictions. My doctoral research explored the connection between health and well-being and our ability to meet our needs in our environment. I focused on these 10 basic human needs.

Most of these needs are self-explanatory—but legitimacy refers to exercising human rights and receiving fair and just treatment, and identity means defining and understanding our personal strengths, limitations, philosophy, and moral values. When our basic human needs are frustrated, we experience fear, anger, sadness, grief, or guilt. As frustration continues, we may turn to addictions in misguided attempts to meet or suppress our basic human needs. When we're unable to meet our needs for extended periods of time, we're prone to stress disorders, frequent viruses, and ultimately, chronic illnesses such as heart disease, diabetes, cancer, and arthritis.

Your Basic Human Needs	
Physical Health	Autonomy
Safety and Security	Predictability and Legitimacy
Love and Affection	
	Recreation
Self-efficacy	Identity
Belonging	Meaning and Hope

Recovery Exercise #3: Your Basic Human Needs While Growing Up and Now.

Use the following questionnaire to assess how well you could meet your basic human needs while growing up and now.

31

Using the following scale, make two ratings about how true each statement is of you, the first when you were 10 years old, and the second at the present time. (Use a 0-10 scale as follows: 0 = very untrue of me, 5 = somewhat true of me and 10 = very true of me.)	Age 10	Now
1. I have good physical health.		
2. I feel safe and secure.		
3. The people close to me love me.		
4. I receive the affection I need from others.		
5. I feel like I am a good and valuable person.		
6. I feel comfortable with important people in my life.		
7. I can improve my life through my own efforts if I wish		
8. What I want is important to those around me.		
9. My life is predictable so I can plan ahead with confidence.		
10. I understand myself well.		
11. I know what is natural and right for me.		
12. I do some enjoyable things just because I want to.		
13. I can relax and forget about my problems at times.		
14. What I do today will make life better for me in the future.		
15. I believe I can have the life I want.		
Your Total Basic Human Needs Scores		

Your Basic Human Need Scores

Your total basic human need scores at age 10 and now can range from 0 to 150. Scores below 60 suggest you endured or currently endure severe need frustration. Scores in the 60-90 range suggest moderate need frustration. Scores in the 90-

120 range suggest moderate need satisfaction. Scores of 120-150 suggest that your needs were or are well met.

If your childhood scores fall below 90, you grew up in an environment without enough resources for you (as you already know). If this was the case, pay special attention to finding a lot of support during recovery through resources such as self-help groups, therapy, close friends, and church and community groups.

Your answers to this questionnaire highlight the needs you were or are most and least able to satisfy. During recovery, make those unmet needs a conscious priority. Think in terms of that little boy or girl inside of you and how you can give back to him or her every day the things they needed then but didn't receive. When you consciously give back to yourself in recovery those things you missed along the way—that inner child will in time repay the care you provide to him or her through the joy, love and spontaneity that are the essential nature of our child selves.

Few families are completely troubled or totally healthy. If we depict family well-being in a bell-shaped curve, the midpoint would represent families with both moderate strengths and moderate problems. About 64 percent of families would fall into this middle range. Approximately 18 percent of families would be very troubled with few resources, and approximately 18 percent would have exceptional resources and well-being.

Family Resources

Families and communities that enhance children's abilities to meet their basic human needs provide protection, affection, stability, support, respect, appropriate freedom, and education to their members. Dolores Curran describes characteristics that are important dimensions of family health (Traits of a Healthy Family):

- The parents love each other and their children.

- Family members talk and listen to each other.

- Family members respect and support each other.

- Family members trust and rely on each other.

- Members shared responsibility reasonably and fairly.

- Family members do things together as a family.

- There are clear family values about right and wrong.

- There are positive family traditions and rituals.

Exceptional Family Health: The Stewarts

Emily and John Stewart spend a few minutes alone with each other before dinner every evening. Married twenty-four years, they maintain a romantic excitement about each other. They carefully give attention to each other and to their five children. John and Emily are often hugging and kissing or have their arms around each other, and John calls Emily "sweetheart." Neighborhood children of all ages love to visit their house to play with the Stewart children. This family seems to have love to spare. Their house is a home base for the children's activities, and there are many comings and goings, but peace prevails.

The Stewarts are not without challenges. Brandon, their third child, developed leukemia and died at age twelve. During his illness, the entire family included and supported Brandon, but each child received attention. At the time of his death, the Stewarts grieved together and individually. They remember Brandon several times each year and visit his grave together.

John and Emily both have strong religious faith, and this helped them face Brandon's death. Although they belong to different churches, they accept this difference in one another peacefully.

Some Stewart children excel in school and others don't, but each member has his or her special distinction in the family for acrobatics, singing, humor, schoolwork, or outdoor activities. The family takes a summer trip each year to a wilderness campground. Everyone pitches in to accomplish the camping tasks. Family members seem to love being who they are as individuals, and each person loves being a "Stewart."

Key Takeaways from This Chapter

- Facing multiple adverse childhood events (ACEs) correlates strongly with our behavioral, health and social problems as adults.

- The family and community resources we can access as children work to offset our difficult childhood experiences.

- The inability to meet certain basic human needs highlights the challenge for many children growing up in troubled family systems.

- Focus during recovery on providing the resources you lacked and meeting basic needs that were not well met while growing up.

- Healthy families provide belonging, recognition, identity, and affection that allow children in those environments to be who they are and thrive.

4. How Troubled Families Wound Children

"Trauma is a fact of life. It does not, however, have to be a life sentence."

Joseph Levine

Characteristics of Troubled Families

In troubled families, we experienced insecurity, distrust, volatility, criticism, conflict, and distance. In many families, problems were hidden or invisible. These hidden family troubles are quite damaging because children don't have dramatic events to explain feelings of distress. Robin Norwood (<u>Women Who Love Too Much</u>) and Dr. Charles Whitfield (<u>Healing the Child Within</u>) identify common characteristics of troubled family environments that gave rise to adult problem behaviors in their books. Here are frequent qualities I have observed in my own and other troubled families.

1. Relationships were unpredictable and contradictory. Relationships in our troubled families often varied dramatically between friendliness and hostility. This included relationships between parents, between parents and children, and between siblings. As children in such families, we found ourselves unable to predict or understand sudden and dramatic shifts in behavior and mood. This undermined our security and ability to trust. A common harmful dimension of unpredictable and contradictory relationships was "psychological abuse," when a parent with character disturbance and/or mental illness sometimes consciously and sadistically manipulates and oppresses a child. Shannon Thomas LCSW describes recovery from psychological abuse in depth in her book (Healing from Hidden Abuse).

Caught in the Middle

Stephanie couldn't rely on being close to either parent for long. Because Stephanie reminded her mother of herself as a girl, her mother was sometimes close and inviting and sometimes critical and cold. Her mother didn't support Stephanie as a teenager when Stephanie was vulnerable and needed compassion. In addition, her mother resented her husband's affection for Stephanie, and Stephanie felt she needed to hide her love for her father. He would then pull back, and Stephanie felt doubly abandoned.

2. Children took adult responsibility. Murray Bowen pointed out that children in troubled families are often assigned to or pulled into adult roles (Family Therapy in Clinical Practice). As children, we lacked the maturity, knowledge, and experience to assume emotional or practical responsibility for other family members, especially parents. Yet, if we perceived that a parent or both parents needed our help, we did our best to make things better by counseling the adults, or becoming an emotional surrogate husband or wife.

No matter how well we may have carried out our "adult" responsibilities, we often came away feeling inadequate. In addition, these responsibilities interrupted our normal developmental tasks.

Trying to Fill His Father's Place

Joshua's father was away a great deal pursuing his career, and Joshua, as the eldest son, became an emotional confidante for his mother. She used Joshua to make up for the lack of support and intimacy she felt in her marriage. Because of their closeness, his mother made excuses for Joshua's school failures and irresponsible spending. Joshua didn't learn to be fully responsible, and his father was extremely critical about this. Joshua felt rejected, but couldn't be close to his father, even though he needed guidance and modeling.

Image 2 portrays one dilemma of a child taking on adult responsibility in a troubled family.

The Reluctant Air Traffic Controller: As children, many of us faced challenging family situations we couldn't handle. We had no choice but to do the best we could to cope with these situations. Here, a child tries to intervene in her parent's conflict without the support, training, understanding, or maturity to take on this very challenging situation. We may have done a competent job in our family, even without resources, but because we lacked real readiness, we always felt anxious and inadequate.

3. Affection and supervision were inappropriate. Some of us, like Joshua, received too much protection, so it inhibited us from developing our own autonomy and responsibility. Others received too little affection and supervision and felt unloved and emotionally deprived. Extreme styles of affection sometimes coexisted within the same parent or parent figure. A parent or older sibling would be affectionate one moment and harsh and angry the next. This inconsistency created an unpredictable and unmanageable childhood environment.

Rejected as a Person

As an adopted child, Rachel felt like an object rather than as a person. When her actions pleased her mother, she was affectionate, but when Rachel went against her mother's authority, her mother rejected her coldly and reminded her she was fortunate to be living in this family. Rachel felt her role was as a showpiece rather than a unique and valuable person. She brought her deep loneliness and need for affection into adulthood. She feared her romantic relationships would never work because in her neediness she looked for a man who could make up for the love she'd missed.

4. We felt emotionally isolated in our families. Dr. Claudia Black (It Will Never Happen to Me) points out that many families have the implicit rule of, "don't talk, don't trust, and don't feel." The result was emotional isolation, and we hesitated to talk to anyone outside our family because there was so much we couldn't talk about. This isolation and distrust remain with us.

Family Secrets

Michael's family had a reputation as a "super family" in his community. The children were highly visible and recognized for both academic and athletic accomplishments. Their home life was a different story, with his mother drinking and his father sometimes suicidal. These family "secrets" were hidden because Michael's father viewed them as evidence of weakness. Secrets added up as the years went on, and Michael couldn't tell his parents he was transsexual. He had reason to fear they wouldn't accept what they would see as a flaw in the family image.

In combination with the above qualities in many of troubled families, other circumstances often aggravated the impact on children and further limited our opportunities to meet basic human needs.

5. There was verbal abuse or physical violence at home. Family verbal abuse or physical violence added significantly to our fear as children. Violence magnified the impact of other destructive factors. The emotional and physical violence some of us encountered included hostile silences, deliberate failure to respond to others' requests, putdowns or sarcasm, name calling and humiliation, intimidation, breaking things, dangerous driving, harsh spanking, pushing, shoving, slapping, and hitting, and, at the extreme, assaulting others with objects, knives, or weapons.

From Abuse to Passivity

Lauren's father beat her mother, who slapped and hit Lauren, particularly as a teenager. Lauren's attractiveness seemed to threaten her mother, who found fault with all Lauren's achievements. When Lauren rebelled, her mother became enraged, and Lauren feared her physical assaults. She learned to be passive about protecting herself and later didn't defend herself when her boyfriend put her down and hit her.

6. Parents were absent because of abandonment, divorce, or death. Losing a parent increased the probability that we wouldn't receive the emotional and physical affection we needed. Parental addiction often co-exists with and amplifies each dimension of family trouble described here. Single parents were emotionally stressed and frequently struggled financially. Divorce exposed some of us to tough choices between loyalty and closeness, and we sometimes felt compelled to ally ourselves with one or the other parent.

A Feeling of Abandonment

Amanda's parents divorced when she was ten, after her alcoholic father abandoned the family. Amanda had been very close to him, so she felt alone and forgotten. Her mother struggled financially for years and never remarried. She resented Amanda, who physically resembled her father and served as a reminder of that painful relationship. Even though she desperately needed affection, Amanda grew up feeling that she couldn't trust anyone.

7. Our families had problems with sexual boundaries. Sexual boundaries, or setting appropriate limits on sexual information, talking, or behavior, are always the responsibility of adults, not children. Dr. Alice Miller notes that children have sexual curiosity but don't engage in adult sexual behavior spontaneously (Thou Shalt Not Be Aware: Society's Betrayal of the Child). Family sexual boundary problems included the absence of appropriate sexual education; inappropriate or humiliating communications to children about sexuality; parental sexual affairs, exposure to pornography, nudity and covert seduction, inappropriate touching, and sexual abuse. In extreme cases, children were victims of sadistic or violent sexual activity. Sexual violations in families have a profound and enduring destructive impact in terms of identity, self-worth, and future sexual behavior.

Confused Sexuality

It horrified Stan as an early teenager when he learned his mother was having an affair. He witnessed his father publicly confronting his mother and her lover, and he felt overwhelmed and humiliated. At that age, he was emotionally unprepared to understand this event. He was naïve about sex and just noticing girls. His mother's affair left him with feeling contempt for women, and he degraded women he became sexual with. It shattered his natural developmental acceptance of sexuality.

8. Parental Addictions and Entrenched Institutional Systems. Parental addiction often co-exists with and amplifies the seven categories of family trouble described above. In addition, the impact of troubled families is greatly magnified for Native Americans, Native Alaskans, Black Americans, and other indigenous peoples and immigrant groups through chronic exposure to, interaction with, and attempts to meet basic human needs within dysfunctional institutions. Trauma including community dysfunction, multigenerational trauma, institutional racism, abuse during boarding school experiences, cultural assault, poverty, lack of opportunity, inadequate education, job training, and health care deficits. The American Psychiatric Association developed guidelines for serving people facing such events (bit.ly/2VeW9pa)

Our Personal Characteristics

Each of us was born with a unique set of personal characteristics, and we experienced a range of sociocultural patterns in our families and communities. Our personal characteristics and the sociocultural setting we experienced can sometimes profoundly affect the overall quality of our childhood environments.

As children, we responded to our parents, and they responded to each of us in individual ways. From birth onward, our temperament and abilities were important in determining how our parents and siblings treated us. Some of us were more demanding than others because of our energy level, strength of will, personality traits, sleeping patterns, or overall physical health.

We assumed that the significant people in our lives were treating us as unique individuals. In troubled families, this was often simply not true. We may have reminded either or both parents of each other, their parents, or other persons with either positive or negative associations, and these associations influenced how they treated us. Frequently we learn later in life that something in a parent's past was important in determining his or her feelings about and treatment of us.

Understanding Her Father's Past

Hannah's father was always distant to her. Once she was a teenager, he no longer showed any affection. This confused

Hannah, and she felt profoundly unworthy because of his rejection. She tried to please her father by her many accomplishments at school, but his coldness was unrelenting.

Later, when Hannah researched her family history, she learned that her father's mother had been mentally ill and had beaten him viciously before the family put her into the state hospital. Hannah recognized her father had unconsciously punished her because of his unresolved childhood rage. Finally, Hannah could stop blaming herself for his rejection, understanding that her father's behavior was that of the hurt and angry little boy within her father.

Cultural Influences on Families

Outside factors can also significantly influence how we fared in our families, including the variety of people we encountered, plus the social, educational, recreational, and cultural resources in our communities. Cultural patterns relating to work, relationships, independence, fun, alcohol and drugs, food, and sex predisposed many of us to specific behavior patterns that began when we were children.

For example, "working hard" and "being kind" are two seemingly worthwhile practices that have led to painful results for some of us who grew up in troubled families. Emphasis on achievement benefits society, but this cultural pattern also contributes to compulsive achievement for some of us with great impact on family relationships or health. Similarly, we're encouraged to be considerate and to help in this culture. But excessive caretaking or attempts to be kind, as in co-dependency, do not achieve what we hope and can lead to negative unintended consequences for ourselves and others.

Key Takeaways from this Chapter

- Troubled families come in many forms, but most include some or all the sources of family troubles described in this chapter.

- Hidden problems are sometimes more difficult for children to cope with because we can't define the sources of our distress.

- Unpredictable relationships with other family members often create a pervasive atmosphere of uncertainty for children.

- The more sources of hurt and instability you faced in your family, the more likely it is that the environment overwhelmed your ability to cope.

- For Black Americans, Native Americans, Native Alaskans and other indigenous families and immigrant groups, multigenerational trauma combined with institutional racism and entrenched dysfunctional community systems multiply the repercussions of family trauma. However, despite this, many people in these communities are now recovering.

5. Ingenious Childhood Survival Strategies

"Refuse to inherit dysfunction. Learn new ways of living instead of repeating what you lived through."

Thema Davis

We find the roots of our problematic adult behavior in the ways we adjusted to our limiting childhood environments. As children, we survived even extreme difficulties, but often at significant emotional cost. Jael Greenleaf points out in her book (Co-Alcoholic, Para-Alcoholic) that as children we had limited power, experience, or information, and didn't have the option of leaving our families. Our need to survive prevailed.

Unconsciously, we carry on the emotional and behavioral strategies that were often ingenious solutions to our childhood predicaments. Our survival strategies may sometimes enhance our adult situations, but frequently create fresh problems. For example, as children, when it was overwhelming to feel the emotional impact of certain events, we shut down our feelings to preserve the illusion that things were okay. As adults, however, when we're out of touch with our emotions, we may ignore critical information needed to guide decisions. When we habitually suppress our emotions, we become emotionally numb. Thus, one important goal in recovery from family trauma is learning to feel again, and moving from illusion-based to self-awareness-based decisions.

Part of our new compassionate perspective on ourselves is accepting that we had to make the best of our difficult childhood situations. This chapter describes the resourceful (although costly) childhood strategies we relied upon.

Childhood Survival Strategies in Troubled Families

Figure 1 presents the aims, behavioral strategies, protective emotional strategies, and self-comforting behavior we developed growing up in troubled family systems. The term "strategy" does not imply that we planned these ways of coping. Our behavior in our troubled family resulted both from being cast in certain roles by the family and from our attempts to make things better. For instance, older children often take responsibility and achieve. As older siblings leave home, younger children may take over these roles.

Child Aims	Behavioral Strategies	Protective Emotional Strategies	Self-Comforting Behavior
Meeting Basic Human Needs such as: Physical Health Safety and Security Love and Affection Self-Worth Etc. Avoiding or improving painful or dangerous situations.	Taking responsibility and achieving Caretaking and controlling in relationships Rebelling or creating problems Adapting or becoming invisible Remaining dependent or under-responsible	Utilizing defense mechanisms Distorting reality self-protectively by suppressing emotions and using the emotional discounting process.	Engaging in satiation behavior such as: Eating Watching TV Engaging in arousal behavior such as: Physical Exertion Risk-taking Masturbation Engaging in fantasy behavior such as: Reading Daydreaming

Sharon Wegscheider-Cruse (<u>Another Chance: Help and Hope for the Alcoholic Family</u>) and Dr. Claudia Black (<u>It Will Never Happen to Me</u>) identified common behavioral strategies in working with alcoholic family systems The following strategies apply to children in many troubled families:

Taking responsibility and achieving

Caretaking and controlling in relationships

Rebelling and being a lightning rod

Adapting or becoming invisible

Remaining dependent or under-responsible

Recovery Exercise # 4: Your Childhood Behavioral Strategies

You may have employed different strategies at different times as your family changed or as older siblings left home. But use the following scales to identify strategies you relied upon most heavily while growing up. Rate each of statement using a 0-10 scale: 0 = very untrue of me, 4 = moderately untrue of me, 6 = slightly true of me, 8 = moderately true of me and 10 = very true of me.

Taking Responsibility and Achieving

My responsibilities as a child went beyond what I could handle.

A major way I felt good about myself was by being responsible.

I tried hard and did well in school or in activities like sports, clubs, or jobs.

I felt like a failure if I didn't do well at something.

Caretaking and Controlling in Relationships

I took (or was assigned) responsibility for other family members as a child.

I counseled or helped one or both of my parents with their problems.

I gave advice or orders to my parents or siblings to make things go better in the family.

I learned to be a good listener, and other people came to me for help.

Rebelling or Being a Lightning Rod

I got in trouble at home because I wouldn't go along with things I thought were wrong.

I raised issues that other family members felt but didn't acknowledge.

I rebelled as a child and did destructive things to me or others.

I got into trouble at school and in the community through acting out.

Adapting and Becoming Invisible

I spent time alone as a child because that was more comfortable than being with my others.

The best thing to do was to keep quiet and let things blow over, so I tried to become invisible.

I hoped someone would seek me out and care about me because I felt so lonely.

Family members acknowledged me for not being a bother, even though I needed more attention.

Remaining Dependent or Under-Responsible

My parents didn't encourage me to become independent and responsible.

One or both of my parents did things for me I needed to do for myself.

Family discipline was loose, and I got away with things I shouldn't have.

I learned to manipulate or con others into doing things for me.

Your Childhood Behavioral Strategy Scores

Add up your scores for each pattern, which can range from 0 to 40. A score of 20 or above shows you strongly relied upon a particular strategy. You'll use this information later as you assess whether your strategies progressed into self-defeating life patterns as an adult.

Protective Emotional Strategies

As children, we had to protect ourselves emotionally to maintain equilibrium as we faced the possibility of emotional abandonment or other family disaster. Our most basic defense as children against painful emotional or environmental developments was to deny them. Dr. Peter Ossorio pointed out, *"If seeing things as they are puts us in an impossible position, we choose not to see things as they are"* (What Actually Happens). By this denial, we bought time (perhaps years) until we could finally understand and integrate those events. Unfortunately, the longer we don't face, understand, and integrate these painful realities, the longer we suffer from them.

Jacqui Lee Schiff clearly described how we use denial as, "emotional discounting" (All My Children). She identified four levels of discounting we used to spare ourselves from confronting potentially devastating emotional situations when we didn't have the resources to face these painful truths:

We discount the <u>existence</u> of a problem.

We discount the <u>significance</u> of a problem, downplaying its <u>intensity</u> or <u>importance</u>.

We discount the <u>possibility of changing</u> a problem.

We discount our <u>own abilities</u> and blame ourselves.

Surviving Fear

Jennifer, a teenager, felt trapped in her family. Her parents fought bitterly and pulled her into their conflicts. Jennifer described these violent scenes in an unemotional manner because she had regularly discounted the intensity and significance of these family crises. She felt helpless to change the situation, and although she wanted to leave home, she felt guilty about leaving behind people she loved. Jennifer criticized herself and concluded she was a burden to her parents and part of the cause of their problems. As a first step in recovery, Jennifer recognized that her parents' problems were of their own making and she couldn't change them. She saw she had discounted her feelings and needs in order to survive. As Jennifer recognized the extent of her fear, she moved in with an aunt and uncle with whom she felt safe.

Unfortunately, we continue to discount feelings after leaving our troubled families. As adults, this discounting contributes to entrapment in unsatisfying situations. As we overcome self-defeating behavior strategies and addictions during recovery, we re-examine past family situations and recognize their true emotional significance. As we develop a new and honest emotional perspective on the past, we're more able to evaluate present situations clearly and act with greater emotional freedom.

Recovery Exercise #5: How You Use Discounting

Identify how you may use discounting in dealing with problems. A good way to do this is to keep a daily log for a week for self-observation. Examine the events of the day and identify times when you discounted your feelings. Also, consider the events of childhood. Today or as a child, did you discount the existence of a problem, discount its intensity or significance, discount the possibilities for change, or discount your own ability and blame yourself?

Be conscious of situations in which you say, "No problem," "I didn't even notice," "That's okay," "No big deal," "I don't care," "There is nothing I can do about it," "I guess I deserved it," or "I can't do anything right." Notice the subtle distress cues you get inside when you discount your feelings. Maybe that bothered you. Maybe there is something you can do about it. Maybe it wasn't your fault. Stopping habitual discounting is part of the *recognition* process that prepares you to take positive action in your life.

As I mentioned in my recovery story in Chapter 2, I discovered my emotional discounting about my childhood family when I joked to therapist colleagues about trying to intervene in my parent's violent arguments, and they responded with silence. Until that moment, I hadn't recognized the emotional significance of what I was saying—but these friends did. I felt humiliated and ashamed, but thankfully this group of people didn't take part in my denial. I was using a psychological defense called "gallows humor" to protect against my genuine feelings by making light of what was a tragic situation. Many children from troubled families use gallows humor, trying to cope with painful and overwhelming family realities.

Self-Comforting Behavior

We comforted ourselves as children using whatever means were available. Drs. Harvey Milkman and Stanley Sunderwirth (Craving for Ecstasy) categorize the self-comforting actions people use into three neuro/psychological categories: satiation, arousal, and fantasy. Sleeping, eating, and watching television are examples of satiation behaviors. Arousal behavior includes intense exciting video games, intense exercising, masturbation, and physical risk-taking. Fantasy behavior includes reading comic books, pulp novels, or daydreaming. The childhood self-comforting strategies we used connect to the kinds of addiction we may turn to as adults.

Recovery Exercise #6: Your Self-Comforting

How did you comfort yourself as a child? Rate the actions below from 0 to 10, with 0 showing low reliance on and 10 showing heavy reliance: eating, sleeping, watching television, physical exercise, video games, masturbation, physical risk taking, reading, daydreaming, and other self-comforting behavior _____?

Becoming Fully Functioning Adults

Because our childhood environments couldn't meet our basic human needs, we used the limited behavioral strategies available. The result was that many of us arrived at adulthood out of balance—compelled to act in certain ways rather than free to be true to ourselves. Compulsion means we continue a specific pattern or habit until it detracts from our well-being and we feel unable to stop. In contrast, freedom means making choices that enhance our best interests. With behavioral freedom, we can achieve a satisfactory balance between four behavior choice perspectives described by Dr. Peter Ossorio: practical, ethical, pleasurable, and tasteful. To explain, let's look at friendship behavior from each of these perspectives.

- We behave practically when we do something realistic and efficient, such as being on time for an appointment with friends or returning a book we borrowed.

- Ethical behavior means doing the right thing rather than cutting corners. In our friendships, we behave ethically when we let other people know honestly where they stand with us.

- Pleasurable behavior is enjoyable for either immediate or symbolic reasons. In friendships, we enjoy sharing meals in pleasant surroundings, and we appreciate the lighthearted exchange about our experiences since we were last together. We feel good when other people communicate clearly that they are our friends.

- Tasteful behavior is pleasing in terms of its sensitivity, excellence, beauty, or eloquence. We're touched when friends remember our birthdays and when they choose gifts to fit with our own interests and tastes.

During recovery we gain the freedom to include a good mix of practicality, ethics, pleasure, and tastefulness in our lives, for example, spending more money than we should, making choices that don't align with our values, doing things we don't want to do, or acting in ways that leave use feeling ashamed. Self-defeating strategies often involve neglecting one or more of these dimensions of behavior choice. Having matured in environments that required survival behavior and didn't allow for balance, we often have growth to complete as we broaden our available choices and learn new and necessary skills. To make these changes, we need alternative support systems and new teachers.

As adults, we can find people who encourage us and provide knowledge and skills we couldn't develop in our childhood families. In creating recovery "families of choice," we take responsibility for our lives and find people who give us what we deeply need. We no longer attempt to force our childhood families to give us what they may not even have to give. This emancipation from our childhood families usually requires facing some loneliness and grief during the separation process, but ultimately can develop relationships with our families that respect who they are and aren't, even if limited.

Image 3 portrays the fact that sometimes we cannot meet our needs in our troubled families.

The Waterhole Gone Dry: A desert scene portrays our sometimes desperate attempts to get the validation, support, protection, and love we wanted from our families of childhood. A dried-up waterhole represents the unfortunate reality that we frequently encounter. There may once have been good water there, or perhaps there was just enough water to allow survival, but now the waterhole is dry. This discouraging reality can weaken us further, but we must save our strength for the task we now face—crossing the desert to the oasis where the validation, support, and resources we need are available.

Key Takeaways from this Chapter

- Children in troubled family systems develop complex and invisible strategies to survive, protect and comfort ourselves, and attempt to improve sometimes dire situations.
- Strategy does not imply volition, but behavioral and emotional solutions (usually unconscious) involving a combination of family roles, emotional defenses, personal characteristics, and sociocultural environments.
- After using these behavioral solutions many times during childhood, we naturally carry them into adulthood and relationships and situations where they do not serve our best interests.
- Thankfully, we now understand and can make visible how these behavioral and emotional patterns develop and continue.
- A central challenge of recovery is revising or replacing strategies that limit our choices or actively harm us. We can accomplish this through the broad resources and support of recovery.

6. Enduring Emotional Adjustments from Childhood

"I grew up in Louisiana, and I grew up in a dysfunctional family with some serious abuse from my stepfather who could be a beautiful person on the one hand and a terrible person on the other, so it leaves your soul troubled as a child."

Tim McGraw

A primary challenge we face on our journey from survival behavior patterns to freedom are three kinds of enduring emotional adjustments stemming from childhood experiences: (1) unstable self-worth, (2) unresolved emotions and post-traumatic stress disorder (PTSD), and (3) difficulty trusting.

These emotional adjustments are distressing, limit our choices, and make us vulnerable to self-defeating life patterns and addictions. During recovery we face these painful emotional states with support and, over time, using new recovery resources, we're able to overcome these painful feelings.

1. Unstable Self-Worth

Unstable self-worth is a subtle and pervasive problem that shows up in many forms: lack of confidence, self-criticism, feelings of unworthiness, perfectionism, grandiosity, withdrawal, self-sabotage, and hesitance to take risks. Many of us are afraid to try anything new because we can't risk humiliation. We find ourselves frequently in a state of anxiety. People in self-help groups describe unstable self-worth as like being "a megalomaniac with an inferiority complex" where we experience dramatic swings between emotional highs and lows.

When we attempt to meet adult challenges and responsibilities with impaired self-worth and a critical internal dialogue, we fear being exposed as inadequate. Shame is one of the most painful dimensions of our unstable self-worth. Gershen Kaufman describes this painful emotion in his book (Shame: The Power of Caring):

"Contained in the experience of shame is the piercing awareness of ourselves as fundamentally deficient in some way as a human being. To live with shame is to experience the very essence or heart of the self as wanting."

To avoid humiliation, we often arrange our lives to avoid this painful exposure at any cost. We practice "image management," emphasizing looking good on the outside regardless of our true emotional or family situation. We put up a good front no matter what, but end up feeling lonely and inadequate. In a society that idolizes and competes for external trappings of success, power, youth, wealth, and happiness, many of us experience a "shame gap." This is the discrepancy between the public image of status, power, confidence, and success we attempt to convey and the private truth about our emotional lives, intimate relationships, and addiction.

Hurting on the Inside

Megan was a successful student who secretly felt unworthy. Her family adopted her as an infant, but she never knew this until a friend told her when she was in high school. Other students then mocked and humiliated Megan. This horrible experience caused deep feelings of hurt, betrayal, and shame. Megan vowed to become a star achiever to show her family and community she was better than they. Her success was empty, however, because underneath her facade she felt deep loneliness and pain. Megan also drank too much and frequently blacked out. Her hidden vulnerability and addiction were inconsistent with the image she tried to convey. When she finally joined Alcoholics Anonymous, Megan could face her pain and learned to validate and respect herself as she was.

There are powerful cultural prohibitions against admitting failure, whether great or small. To recover, however, we must overcome image management and shame. We confront with compassion the truth about ourselves, our lives, and our families as we grow toward well-being. The ingredients of compassion are (1) understanding the powerful family forces that shaped us; (2) recognizing that other people struggle with similar dilemmas, and (3) embracing the hope that we can change our lives for the better.

Recovery Exercise #7: Your Self-Worth

Use a 0-10 Scale, where 10 is "very true" about you.

I can do what I must do to improve my life.

I give myself the benefit of the doubt when I make mistakes.

I feel worthy as a person.

I'm able to try new things without doing them perfectly.

I feel good about how I meet my responsibilities.

How I appear to others matches my feelings inside.

I feel compassion for myself and my life.

I don't experience big mood swings regularly.

Starting Repair of Your Self-Worth

Your score on this scale can range from 0 to 80. A score of 40 or below suggests that unstable self-worth may be a significant challenge for you. If your score is between 40 and 60, you have moderately stable self-worth. A score between 60 and 80 suggests you have stable self-worth. If you have unstable or moderately stable self-worth, a good way to change this is through practicing kindness to yourself. Using a book of daily affirmations really helps. Each positive recovery choice and action you take adds slightly to your self-worth.

---

2. Unresolved Emotions and Post-Traumatic Stress Disorder (PTSD)

Like Megan, we may carry unresolved feelings of hurt, disappointment, shame, guilt, loss, anger, or grief from the past. We may not have had the safety and opportunity before now to process the emotional impact of important events of both childhood and adulthood. Feeling unloved or unwanted, experiencing constant conflict, the death or loss of a parent or sibling, family violence, and sexual boundary problems can each create deep emotional wounds, but because we learned to discount the emotional impact of these traumas to protect ourselves, we never faced them.

When we view reality through the defensive shield of discounting, we become emotionally numb with frozen feelings. We either don't allow ourselves to feel anything, or we prevent ourselves from feeling too deeply because we're afraid we'll fall apart. Often, we may become hypersensitive to rejection, conflict, anger, inconsistency, or sexuality. Many of us feel unable to cope with life events that naturally involve setbacks, losses, transitions, challenging emotions, and conflicts. We perceive normal experiences as insurmountable and may conclude our situations are hopeless.

An important task for young adults is to become independent of our childhood families and learn to function in the larger world—sometimes a frightening experience. To postpone leaving home, some of us made rather desperate attempts to change our families for the better, not accepting we couldn't make them change. After leaving home, we had to learn the difference between rebelling against and being independent of our families. Some of us try desperately not to be like our parents and as the result discard strengths our families provided. Such rebellion reflects our unfinished separation. True separation frees us to choose ways of life that truly suit us.

A Continuum of Traumatic Experiences

The painful experiences children and adults face in troubled families fall on a continuum between difficult life experiences and severe traumatic events. The more severe the experience, the more extreme is the impact. Unfortunately, in some troubled families, children, and adults experience, sometimes over and over, extreme and violent events. The term Post-Traumatic Stress Disorder (PTSD) originally described how people react to extreme events, such as combat, natural catastrophes, or sexual assault. We now know that less dramatic events (particularly repeated events) can also result in PTSD. The mental health diagnostic manual (<u>Diagnostic and Statistical Manual of Mental Disorders-V</u>) identifies the criteria for PTSD in response to trauma as:

(a) experiencing or witnessing either a life-threatening event or a threat to the personal integrity of oneself or others, and (b) accompanied by the experience of perceived intense fear, helplessness, or horror.

We diagnose PTSD when these symptoms continue for more than a month after the actual events. When people face this kind of threat, we have a fight/flight/freeze response. These physiological responses are the body's attempt to adapt and survive, including a higher heart rate, shallow breathing, and slowing digestion. These autonomic responses prepare the body to survive the physical threat, but emotionally laden memories often emerge later.

Complex PTSD (C-PTSD)

Dr. Judith Lewis Herman introduced the concept of complex PTSD in 1992 to describe the physical and psychological aftermath of people exposed to severe trauma over a long period, not merely in a single incident. Her paper reviewed multiple studies of devastating consequences for survivors of severe situations such as people held in captivity, tortured, and survivors of concentration camps (<u>bit.ly/3dg4Vs6</u>). She noted several important long-term effects that manifested in such survivors:

> "Clinical observations identify three broad areas of disturbance which transcend simple PTSD. The first is symptomatic: the symptom picture in survivors of prolonged trauma often appears to be more complex, diffuse, and tenacious than in simple PTSD. The second is characterological: survivors of prolonged abuse develop characteristic personality changes, including deformations of relatedness and identity. The third area involves the survivor's vulnerability to repeated harm, both self-inflicted and at the hands of others."

Many of us who grew up in troubled environments can identify with some characteristics that Dr. Herman identified—(a) diffuse somatic, psychological, and behavioral symptoms, (b) character changes in relationships and identity, and (c) vulnerability to repeated harm either self-inflicted or by others. In my personal recovery and professional experience, this explains why many of us seeking professional help have discovered that single psychotherapy approaches are often insufficient and sometimes destructive because when we couldn't find relief, we were prone to increased self-doubt and despair.

Recovering from family trauma and adverse childhood experiences is a whole person, whole life endeavor. Our multiple symptoms of distress are successfully addressed and overcome using the comprehensive array of psychotherapy, self-help, self-care, and specialized trauma resolution approaches now available, which I describe in Chapter 9.

General Adaptation Syndrome

Dr. Hans Selye (1907-1982) is considered the father of our understanding of stress and its profound connection to well-being and health. In his early research work with lab animals subjected to chronic distress from which they could not escape, he described a predictable process these unfortunate creatures went through which he termed "General Adaptation Syndrome (bit.ly/2P4foAH).

> "Selye's proposal stipulated that stress was present in an individual throughout the entire period of exposure to a nonspecific demand. He distinguished acute stress from the total response to chronically applied stressors, terming the latter condition 'general adaptation syndrome', which is also known in the literature as Selye's Syndrome. The syndrome divides the total response from stress into three phases: the alarm reaction, the stage of resistance and the stage of exhaustion."

Consistent with Dr. Herman's description of C-PTSD above, Dr. Selye's *General Adaptation Syndrome* identifies a complex series of physiological and psychological reactions that take place when people or animals are subjected to chronic distress from which they cannot escape—exactly the situation in which many children find themselves in with their families, often for years. This further validates the research reviewed earlier regarding the long-term behavioral, psychological and health correlates of Adverse Childhood Experiences (ACEs).

I mentioned early in this book that "recovery does not mean as good as new." What I've learned during my life and in working with many other people who grew up in challenging backgrounds is that we can attain levels of well-being that we never thought possible, but most of us will never recover a tolerance for placing ourselves in situations or around people which touch old wounds. I discuss this in more depth later in Chapters 14 and 15 dealing with *Creating Relationships that Support Recovery* and *Maintaining Your Recovery*.

Reminders Trigger Past Traumatic Memories

When we face extreme situations, we store in memory images, sounds and emotions and a play-by-play account of these events. Because our brain can't take in overwhelming information during extreme trauma, it stores aspects of the event in memory like fragmented pieces of broken glass. When we recall these events, these memories can rush back to awareness and we see, hear, feel, and re-experience exactly what we went through. Situations that sound, look, feel, or smell like the original event trigger memories, thoughts, and feelings that we react to automatically. The common element of these triggered memories is emotional arousal and fear, signaling that the traumatic event is still happening.

When we get triggered by a particular person, sight, sound, smell, or color, it activates each fragmented part of the traumatized memory. Our fight/flight/freeze response may precipitate a panic attack, or we may become immobilized or lash out. The experience can be overwhelming. Even if your experience was less severe than the criteria of extreme trauma above, you may develop PTSD-like symptoms, including the following characteristics.

- **Avoidance:** We avoid situations and people that trigger us in various ways—by not remembering, feeling detached, numb, or estranged from others, or losing interest in activities we formerly enjoyed. We strive not to re-experience the feelings, thoughts, or body sensations arising when we think about the traumatic situation. We may feel guilty, ashamed, or terrified when we're reminded of the trauma.

- **Re-experiencing the event:** The sensory dimensions of a traumatic event can seem to pop out of nowhere, reminding us that the memory is alive and well, except our reaction is out of proportion to the current situation. Flashbacks, sounds, thoughts, memories, and perceptions may arise unexpectedly and we feel like we're going through the event again. Many people have dreams and nightmares similar to the event and feel intense emotional and physical distress.

Beginning PTSD and Trauma Recovery

Comprehensive and effective recovery strategies are now available for both PTSD and for less severe traumatic events children often experience growing up in troubled families. Two effective workbooks for overcoming PTSD are from Dr. Arielle Schwartz, (A Practical Guide to Complex PTSD: Compassionate Strategies to Begin Healing Childhood Trauma), and Dr. Mary Beth Williams (PTSD Workbook: Effective Techniques for Overcoming Traumatic Stress Symptoms).

In Chapter 9, *A Wealth of Resources for Recovery*, I describe two powerful therapy resources for moving beyond trauma— multi-modal experiential therapy and Eye Movement Desensitization and Reprocessing (EMDR). With effective treatment and support, we're able to put our painful and traumatic experience into the proper perspective. Processing and understanding such painful experiences allow us to move on with our lives and integrate painful memories. With healing, these will always be unfortunate or even tragic memories, but they no longer have the power to dominate our lives.

Recovery Exercise #8: Your Unresolved Emotions and PTSD

Use a 0-10 Scale, where 10 means "very true" about you.

1. I went through experiences growing up (or in adulthood) that I haven't let myself feel.

2. I overreact emotionally to situations that touch old feelings.

3. I'm better off not expecting too much, so I won't get disappointed if things don't work out.

4. I become depressed, angry, or fearful without really understanding why.

5. I don't understand what I really feel and need.

6. I avoid people who remind me of others from the past.

7. I'm afraid to let myself feel too deeply because I might fall apart.

8. I try to avoid situations that might trigger old memories.

Unresolved Emotions and PTSD Total

Your score on this scale can range from 0 to 80. Any single item scored at 7 or above suggests an issue to deal with during recovery. An overall score below 25 suggests that unresolved emotions may not deeply trouble you. A score of

25-50 implies unresolved feelings moderately interfere with your life. A score of 50 or above suggests significant distress, and it may be helpful to see a professional for support with unresolved feelings.

Image 4 portrays our enduring emotional adjustments from childhood.

Healing Our Inner Children: An old-fashioned camera reveals the little boy or girl hidden behind our adult trappings of affluence and success. We must reconcile ourselves with these inner children who carry the memories of childhood losses, hurts, and disappointments. As our inner children heal, they release the tremendous resources of our childhood selves. Then, we rediscover the spontaneity, humor, creativity, tenderness, and love that are the natural experiences of childhood.

3. Difficulty Trusting Ourselves and Others

Singly or in combination, unstable self-worth, unresolved emotions, and PTSD limit our ability to trust ourselves, others, and the world at large. Many of us grow up not believing we can create meaningful lives, form lasting and satisfying relationships, and find a fulfilling place for ourselves in the world. We may enter romantic relationships fearing abandonment. We become preoccupied with image management and shame about our histories and inner lives, and create an invisible distance from other people, who feel pushed away and then withdraw. Thus, we end up alone, telling ourselves we knew all along this would happen and must deserve it.

Acting from unstable self-worth, we sometimes enter and remain in relationships with people who don't treat us well. We don't know how to resolve relationship conflicts because we're afraid of anger, lack awareness of our needs, and find it hard to express our feelings honestly. Unfinished separation from our childhood families drains the energy we have for adult relationships. The combined result of these emotional adjustments is that we often live in a state of fear. Dr. Peter Ossorio describes our basic fear is, *"This world doesn't have a place for me, as me."* (What Actually Happens: The Representation of Real-World Phenomena).

Dr. Patrick Carnes describes three core beliefs that underlie all addictive behaviors (Out of the Shadows: Understanding Sexual Addiction):

- I am basically a bad, unworthy person.

- No one would love me as I am.

- My needs will never be met if I must depend on others.

Beginning to Trust

With such desperate feelings inside, we enter adulthood determined to escape our childhood dragons. Many of us absorb many painful life experiences before accepting we must ultimately confront these feelings we fear. Discovering we can connect through self-help groups with many other people who have been through experiences like our own brings us into the human fold. We don't have to face our dragons alone, and with the support of these recovery allies, we never have to be alone and hopeless with our pain again.

Ryan's Emancipation

Ryan met a woman he liked after college but in describing himself said: "I don't trust my decisions. I feel bad about how I'm running my life. My self-worth is poor. My family was strict, and I didn't develop my own ideas. My parents didn't approve of anything I did, so I rebelled inside, but I went along with what they wanted for me because inside I felt lost. They wanted me to become a lawyer, but I'm not cut out for that. I'm more interested in being a writer."

Ryan's Enduring Emotional Adjustments

Ryan felt debilitated by this childhood environment of rejection and criticism. He needed support, guidance, and trust as he sought to become independent and find his appropriate place in the world, but felt that he had to adapt and become invisible to survive in his family.

He comforted himself by retreating into books and daydreams, and his interest in being a writer grew out of these childhood activities. He used marijuana to retreat into fantasy when life seemed too painful. As a young adult, Ryan didn't know himself well and hadn't gained confidence through trial-and-error decision making. Ryan yearned to trust his feelings about what was right for him, but he needed support.

Ryan's Healing Process

As he recovered, Ryan learned to be compassionate with himself about the process of his life. "I did pretty well, even though my parents didn't accept me. I'm ready to move on and have the life I want." As a starting place, he discontinued all drug use. Later, he chose friends who supported him being true to himself. He recognized he needed acceptance and appreciation from his family of choice.

At work, Ryan recognized he expected people to treat him the way they had treated him at home. By presenting himself in a self-depreciating way, he inadvertently set himself up for this. As he felt better about himself, he presented himself more confidently at work and people respected him. Ryan pursued the woman he was interested in with his eyes open, with no illusion she could offset his past hurts. As his new life took shape and his parent's inability to accept him no longer preoccupied Ryan, he stopped resenting their failings and created a support system that validated who he was.

Key Takeaways from this Chapter

- Internalized childhood failures and disappointments manifest themselves as unstable self-worth.

- Painful and traumatic events with lasting aftermath unfortunately characterize many troubled families.

- Unresolved emotions and PTSD perpetuate our vulnerability, and we often become emotionally numb or emotionally reactive.

- Specific people, sights, sounds, smells and colors can trigger painful flashbacks that plunge us into fight/flight/freeze responses.

- Difficulty trusting ourselves and others increases our sense of isolation and makes it hard to receive support when we most need it.

7. Self-Defeating Life Patterns

"Growth is painful. Change is painful. But nothing is as painful as staying somewhere you don't belong."

Mandy Hale

"I won't make the mistakes my parents made," many of us say to ourselves as we launch into adulthood. With the natural optimism of youth, we apply our energy and strength to achieving "success" and "happiness." Unfortunately, what we sometimes create instead are self-defeating life patterns that can sabotage adult well-being and success. These self-defeating patterns flow directly from childhood survival strategies, which we don't stop until we're locked in and they negatively affect our relationships and physical and emotional health.

How Self-Defeating Life Patterns Develop

Self-defeating life patterns derive directly from our childhood behavioral strategies:

- Taking responsibility and focusing on achieving can lead to compulsive achievement.

- Caretaking and controlling in relationships can lead to co-dependency. Robin Norwood originally described co-dependency in <u>Women Who Love Too Much</u>.

- Rebelling and being a lightning rod can lead to generalized rebellion.

- Adapting and becoming invisible can lead to casualty syndrome.

- Remaining dependent under-responsible may lead to under-responsibility pattern.

These adult behavior patterns involve <u>over-using</u> our childhood coping mechanisms. How do these activities become self-defeating behavior strategies? Dr. Claudia Black points out that for each child survival strategy, we learn certain skills, but simultaneously neglect others (<u>It Will Never Happen to Me</u>). For example, if we learn to take responsibility and achieve, we may not learn to ask for help and trust. If we learn to be dependent or under-responsible, we may not learn how to take care of ourselves or follow through with commitments. Childhood patterns become self-defeating life patterns as we use the skills we have over and over, while neglecting other skills we need to develop. The wider the "skill gap" becomes, the more challenging it becomes to learn the skills we've unwittingly neglected.

There's an ironic trait of human nature at work here. When a particular strategy doesn't seem to work anymore, our first reaction is to use it even more frequently and more intensely. For example, when we encounter someone who doesn't treat us fairly, we may become angry. When this doesn't seem to change their behavior toward us, we become more aggressive and more demanding, perhaps shouting and making threats.

Or, we may respond to mistreatment by being increasingly accommodating, failing to notice that we're dealing with someone who isn't acting in good faith. Recovery involves identifying our misguided strategies and substituting new behavior options, including the option to walk away from a situation or relationship that is toxic for us.

By early adulthood, our behavioral strategies and skill deficits have become established and habitual. Our choices become habits, these habits become our reality, and through this reality we define ourselves and the world. In this way, we become deeply invested in remaining the same, even if that means remaining in pain and conflict. Unfortunately, many of us conclude that unhappiness and conflict are normal and unavoidable.

As adults, we sometimes make broad statements about ourselves such as, "I'm good at getting things done, so I might as well do it myself," or, "I'm afraid to tell him/her what I want because they'll laugh at me," or, "I don't understand men (women)," or, "I hate being told what to do," or, "I'm shy in new situations," or "Why should I do it if I can get someone to do it for me?" We don't question how these beliefs developed; we just assume that's the way we are.

Three factors explain why we perpetuate certain child behavior strategies into adulthood, where they progress into self-defeating life patterns.

We have a mistaken belief (relating to childhood circumstances) that this behavior will lead to achieving our goals.

Each behavior pattern leads to intermittent rewards that reinforce the pattern.

Continuing our survival behavior helps us to avoid recognizing painful feelings and problems.

As self-defeating life patterns progress, we over-invest in these behaviors and under-invest in behavior that would help us meet other basic human needs. We may dimly recognize the psychological, physical, and interpersonal complications resulting from our choices, but because our strategies sometimes work, we hesitate to change. As we continue using our childhood survival behavior patterns, we create increasingly unbalanced adult situations.

For many of us who grew up in families challenged with trauma and addiction, one self-defeating life pattern may create the most problems, but some of us also have characteristics of other patterns. For instance, we may be compulsive achievers in professional life but behave according to under-responsibility pattern in an intimate relationship.

Five Self-Defeating Life Patterns

During the behavior change process in recovery, *clarity* means we understand exactly how specific problem behaviors and complications work, which enables us to address these one by one. Each self-defeating life pattern has four important characteristics:

The <u>primary behavior</u> that defines the pattern,

The <u>central obsession</u> that preoccupies us with this pattern,

The <u>mistaken belief</u> that perpetuates the pattern, and

The <u>missing skills</u> that make the pattern difficult to change.

Following the description of each pattern below, you'll assess whether that pattern is a problem for you.

1. Compulsive Achievement

Primary behavior: involvement in sports, school, and work over sixty hours per week; considering one's achievements as a primary identity; working to achieve when you need to spend time with family or friends; neglecting health or rest to advance personal goals.

Central obsession: thinking about, planning for, or worrying about achievement when not actively striving.

Mistaken belief: When I meet my next goal, I'll be happy.

Missing skills: the ability to relax during unstructured time, and the capability to be emotionally close.

Under-Investing in Himself

"I know that my marriage is in trouble. My wife says I spend too many hours at work. I just don't feel close to her anymore. She doesn't seem to understand what I have to do to get ahead at my job and seems angry all the time."

As a self-employed regional sales representative, Justin thought constantly about the money he made the more hours he worked. As a child, he'd struggled in school and felt humiliated. When he discovered his sales ability, it was a tremendous boost to his self-worth, and he devoted more and more time to succeeding. He began spent evenings and weekends making phone calls to lining up appointments.

The result of Justin's overinvestment in work was underinvestment in his marriage and family relationships, in caring for his health, and in recreation. His business success was becoming meaningless because he'd neglected these other aspects of his life. He suffered from migraine headaches and stomach problems. As time went on, Justin became less able to withdraw mentally from thinking or planning for work. He couldn't wait for the weekend to be over and get back on the road. He smoked two packs of cigarettes a day and relied on alcohol to unwind and fall asleep at night.

Justin's mistaken belief was "If I'm successful in sales I'll be happy!" Work provided self-worth, and recognition, status, and financial success. Justin's childhood motivation was an unconscious statement to those who had humiliated him: "I'll show you I'm somebody!" His constant activity allowed him to avoid feelings of emptiness and loneliness and distracted him from the increasing consequences of his compulsive achievement. The more desperate these consequences became, the more compelled Justin felt to offset them with even greater professional achievements.

Image 5 portrays the childhood decision of a compulsive achiever who denies himself other necessary aspects of life because of relentless striving.

Compulsive Achiever: It's Sunday afternoon and the compulsive achiever is preparing diligently for the coming week. He feels sad at passing up weekend fun, but considers the demands of work too pressing to allow time for any frivolous activity. He's making another payment toward the long-term price of compulsive achievement—isolation, fatigue, and deprivation.

Recovery Exercise #9: Compulsive Achievement Self-Assessment

If compulsive achievement is a pattern in your life, rate how the characteristics of the pattern apply to you. Use a 0-10 scale for each characteristic, where 0 = very untrue of me, 4 = moderately untrue of me, 6 = moderately true of me, and 10 = very true of me.

1. I engage in school, sports, and work over sixty hours per week.

2. My achievements are my primary identity.

3. I work, work out or study even when I know I need to spend time with family or friends.

4. I neglect my health or rest trying to achieve my goals.

5. I think about, plan for, or worry about achieving when I'm not actively working.

6. I equate happiness with my level of achievement.

7. It's hard for me to relax during unstructured time.

8. It's hard for me to be emotionally close.

Your Compulsive Achievement Score

The highest possible score on this self-assessment is 80. Single-item high scores or an overall score above 40 suggest you may have a problem with this pattern.

2. Co-Dependency

Primary behavior: investing time, energy, and affection in an intimate relationship with someone who doesn't reciprocate equally; subordinating one's own wishes, needs, and values to accommodate a partner; taking most or all the responsibility for the problems in a relationship; worrying more about the other person's problems than he or she worries about him or herself.

Central obsession: thinking, worrying, or planning how to improve a relationship.

Mistaken belief: If I care for someone enough, they will care about me.

Missing skills: awareness of personal feelings and needs; ability to protect oneself from criticism or abuse.

Fear of Being Alone

Ashley was depressed, anxious, and angry and often sick. Her husband Rick didn't reciprocate her caring. He frequently criticized Ashley and gave her little affection or attention. She extended herself more and more to please him, trying to be attentive and considerate of his needs, and tried to inspire him to be the romantic partner she wished for.

From time to time, Ashley became extremely frustrated and lashed out at Rick. In response to her explosions, he became attentive for a time, but then seemed to pull away even more. The possibility of losing Rick terrified Ashley, and in response to his distance, she would soon begin "caretaking" again.

As time went on, Ashley spent more time and energy preoccupied with and worried about her relationship. She encouraged Rick to read books or talk to their minister, but he wouldn't follow through. She gradually withdrew from her friendships and social activities. She felt ashamed she didn't have the loving relationship she craved. She comforted herself with junk food until she was 40 pounds overweight.

Ashley's mistaken belief was, "I can love him enough to make him love and care for me." Rick had grown up in a cold household and didn't learn to be tender and giving. In the early phases of the relationship, he responded to Ashley, and off and on was sensitive and interested. Ashley lived for these intermittent rewards, but she was emotionally starving in the relationship.

The childhood motivation behind Ashley's behavior was rejection by her father and determination to make another man "love me and see how special I am." Her loneliness, anger, and fear frightened her because they triggered powerful childhood feelings of hopelessness and self-hatred.

She tried desperately to make her marriage work in order to avoid facing painful reality.

<u>Image 6</u> presents the discrepancy between the romantic visions that couples may unknowingly carry into a love relationship.

His Dream/Her Dream: The romantic couple is lost in the euphoria of "being in love." Each partner envisions a person who will fulfill their needs for attention and caring. His vision is of a woman who caters to his every wish. Her vision is of romance and an intimate life together. Both envision themselves receiving. Eventually, the discrepancy between their visions becomes apparent.

Recovery Exercise #10: Co-Dependency Self-Assessment

If co-dependency may be a problem for you, rate to what extent the characteristics below apply to you using the same 0-10 scale you used for the compulsive achievement self-assessment.

1. I invest time, energy, and affection in a relationship where these qualities aren't reciprocated equally.

2. I subordinate my own wishes, needs, and values to accommodate a partner.

3. I take more than my share of responsibility for the problems in a relationship.

4. I worry more about another person's problems than he/she does.

5. I spend much of my time thinking, planning, or worrying about how to improve the relationship.

6. I try directly or indirectly to change another adult's feelings and behavior toward me.

7. It's difficult to identify and express my feelings and needs.

8. I feel unable to protect myself from criticism or abuse.

Your Co-Dependency Score

The total possible score on this scale is 80. High single-item scores or an overall score above 40 suggest that you may have a problem with this pattern.

Generalized Rebellion

Primary behavior: engaging in uninvited attempts to influence people and organizations; frequently taking a scapegoat or "fall guy" role in group situations; taking responsibility for things that are not appropriately your concern; using gentler persuasion at first, then turning to more aggressive tactics when others do not respond.

Central obsession: outrage over the irresponsibility or misbehavior of people or organizations.

Mistaken belief: "My good intentions and efforts can overcome any problem.

Missing skills: ability to let issues pass without challenge if they don't directly involve you; ability to disengage from people or situations you can't change.

A Frustrating Campaign

"I'm so upset about work I can't sleep. I took a job as an assistant manager in this office supply company a year ago. I was excited about the job but can't stand the infighting and favoritism. They made a guy who started after me the manager for the evening shift. It drives me crazy!"

Joseph began a fruitless struggle to institute changes at work, even though some of his concerns weren't his responsibility. People listened to his initial suggestions, but as time went on, they stopped listening and they considered him a troublemaker.

Because of his campaigns over various issues, Joseph didn't fulfill his own duties completely, and it strained his relationships with other staff members. He took his work frustration home and had more conflicts with his family. He wasn't enjoying life, and he spent evenings smoking, drinking, and watching TV.

Joseph's mistaken belief was, "I know how things could be better here and I can bring these changes about if I try hard enough." His intermittent success at instituting changes was rewarding enough to give him a sense of autonomy and self-esteem.

The roots of Joseph's present struggle were in his childhood attempts to change his family. For years, he tried to change his parent's conflicts and stop their arguments over money. His unconscious childhood resolve was "I'll make my family change, no matter what!" As Joseph confronted his failure to change his place of employment, he recognized his long-standing frustration about his inability to help his family.

Image 7 portrays our long-term failure at changing painful realities that are not under our control.

The Lost Cause Graveyard: A graveyard is the appropriate resting place for many of the issues we fight in generalized rebellion. As adults, we unwittingly choose people and situations we were powerless to change, thus duplicating the limitations of our childhood environment. We can't make other people and organizations be what we want and need.

Recovery Exercise #11: Generalized Rebellion Self-Assessment

Have you struggled with lost causes and situations you were powerless to change? If so, use the 0-10 scale to rate the extent to which the following characteristics apply to you.

1. I engage in uninvited attempts to influence people and organizations.

2. I take the scapegoat or "fall guy" role in group situations.

3. I take responsibility for things that aren't appropriately my concern.

4. I use gentler persuasion at first and then turn to more aggressive tactics when others don't respond.

5. I'm preoccupied with the irresponsibility or misbehavior of people or organizations.

6. I believe I can overcome any problem with good intentions and effort.

7. I can't let issues pass without challenge, even if they don't directly involve me.

8. It's hard to disengage emotionally, even when it's clear I can't directly influence people and situations.

Your Generalized Rebellion Score

The total possible score is 80. Single high scores or an overall score of 40 or above imply that you have a problem with this pattern.

Casualty Syndrome

Primary behavior: taking part naively or passively in situations that affect your well-being; trying to get other people to take care of you; expressing hostility passively or indirectly; letting authority figures such as parents, professionals, or church authorities tell you what's best for you.

Central obsession: preoccupation with how others have wronged you.

Mistaken belief: If I just do what is right, other people will as well.

Missing skills: awareness of your feelings and needs; ability to assert your wishes and rights.

Just Doing Her Job

"I feel defeated. I can't cope with life. We moved to this town three years ago, after my father abandoned us. He was violent with my mother and older brother, and when she went to the safe house, he left us. Since that time, we've had a hard time getting back on track."

Elizabeth was pale and showed little emotion as she described her life. She had responsibility after school for her three younger siblings, and she worked at a Quick-Stop that didn't allow her to use her capabilities. After her father left, the family was in constant financial stress and her mother made things worse by spending money on furnishings they couldn't afford.

Elizabeth tried to hold the family together, but her father had never fully accepted career and financial responsibilities, and turned to alcohol as an escape. Until her mother finally drew the line conflict, violence, and frequent crisis characterized their lives. The family lived on a roller coaster of financial challenges, conflict, and unhappiness. Elizabeth's childhood hope was, "If I just go along quietly and do my part, things will turn out all right."

Recovery Exercise #12: Casualty Syndrome Self-Assessment

If you feel victimized in a relationship or job situation, rate which characteristics of casualty syndrome you experience in that situation. Use the 0-10 scale.

1. I take part passively in situations that directly affect me.
2. I hope to find someone who'll take care of me.
3. I let people know indirectly when I'm unhappy about something.
4. I allow authority figures in my life to tell me what is best for me.
5. I dwell on how people have wronged me.
6. I believe that if I do what's right, other people also will.
7. It's hard to identify my feelings and needs.
8. I don't know how to assert my own rights and wishes.

Your Casualty Syndrome Score

The highest possible score is 80. Single high scores or an overall score above 40 imply that you may have a problem with this pattern.

Under-Responsibility Pattern

Primary behavior: not following through on your commitments; getting others to take care of your responsibilities; asking that people make allowances for you or your special circumstances or limitations; finding that others are often angry or disappointed in you because of your behavior.

Central obsession: trying to find an easier way.

Mistaken beliefs: If I can get away with it or get someone to do it for me, I might as well. You shouldn't have to work too hard in life.

Missing skill: taking responsibility for oneself.

Charming His Way through Life

"My wife and I separated when she discovered I was having an affair for a year. I knew I had to stop seeing the other woman, but couldn't break things off. Things aren't going well in my business, either. I started it about three years ago and it grew faster than I expected. I overspent and got behind with the IRS. Now I can't get out of debt."

Jacob was an attractive and obviously talented person, and his charisma drew others to him. Many people had given him the benefit of the doubt in the past, but now their trust was wearing thin. Jacob's pattern was letting things deteriorate before attempting to solve the problem. His new starts lasted for a short time before he'd neglect responsibilities and undermine his progress.

Jacob's mistaken belief was "If I really try hard for a while, then I can relax." As the youngest child in his family, his mother made excuses for Jacob and protected him from the consequences of his irresponsibility. He learned his charm would get him through. The intermittent rewards of being irresponsible came from other people tolerating his lack of follow through on commitments, at least for a time.

Jacob's childhood decision behind this behavior came from with his relationship with his father, who didn't push Jacob to achieve or require hard work and follow through. Jacob's conclusion became, "I don't have to push myself and can just do enough to get by."

By the time Jacob went through his cycle many times, he felt intermittently desperate. He turned to sexual affairs to relieve his distress and as a result sowed the seeds of his next crisis.

Recovery Exercise #13: Under-Responsibility Pattern Self-Assessment

Do you have some characteristics of under-responsibility pattern? Rate which characteristics apply to you using the 0-10 scale.

1. It's hard to meet my commitments.
2. I let other people take care of things that are really my responsibility.
3. People make allowances for me or my special circumstances or limitations.
4. I find myself in trouble with others because of my behavior.
5. I think about how to avoid the drudgery of life.
6. If I can get away with something or get someone else to do it, I might as well.
7. I shouldn't have to work too hard in life.
8. It's hard to take full responsibility for myself.

Your Under-Responsibility Pattern Score

The highest possible score on this scale is 80. Single high scores or an overall score of 40 or above imply that you may have a problem with this pattern.

Complications of Our Self-Defeating Strategies

Understanding how self-defeating life patterns apply to you gives you a clear focus for behavior change. Thinking about how each pattern may apply for you helps you be clear about your blend of these behaviors. This understanding will help you in moving from survival behavior to freedom.

This chapter described five people actively struggling with self-defeating life patterns which did not serve their best interests, but operated invisibly so they couldn't readily identify where they were going wrong. Their lives illustrate common complications of self-defeating behavior strategies:

- Neglect of self-care, diet, and exercise

- Getting sick frequently

- Muscle tension and pain

- Shame, guilt, anger, or disappointment

- Depression, anxiety, or insomnia

- Family or marital conflict

- Work conflict

- Burnout symptoms such as cynicism, apathy, or fatigue

In Chapter 8, you'll evaluate the severity of these complications in your life and develop a plan to address these complications.

Key Takeaways from this Chapter

- Adult self-defeating life patterns derive from childhood family roles and survival patterns and the faulty beliefs which sustain them.

- We develop these coping strategies which unwittingly perpetuate the limitations and frustrations of our childhood environments.

- Each pattern provides some intermittent reinforcement which leads to more entrenched reliance on these strategies.

- Many of us have some characteristics of several self-defeating life patterns.

- Over time, these patterns are progressively less successful and can lead to significant emotional, health and relationship consequences.

8. From Escape to Addiction

"Addictions represent misguided spiritual yearning."
Unknown

As human beings, we naturally seek changes in consciousness. Achieving a satisfying and lasting state of mind and body is a basic life challenge. Our feelings and awareness can change subtly or dramatically, sometimes rapidly and sometimes gradually. We achieve subtle changes in consciousness by taking a hot shower in the morning, eating a delicious meal, completing a project at work, watching a beautiful sunset, working out at our health club, or playing with children in the evening. More dramatic changes in consciousness come from drinking alcohol, using drugs, over- and under-eating, having sex, risk taking, or gambling.

The more distress we experience, the more likely we are to seek distinct and immediate changes in consciousness. These behavior patterns become addictive when we choose them over and over until we feel unable to stop, even when we harm ourselves or others. Our addictive escapes create significant new emotional, health and relationship problems.

Potential Addictions Are Everywhere

Emotional, biological, family, and cultural factors all contribute to the development of addiction. For many of us, pain resulting from enduring emotional adjustments and self-defeating life patterns increases the probability that we will seek relief through escapes. Families, communities, and society all teach us about different escapes. Our parents modeled "appropriate" escapes, and as children and teenagers we made discoveries about escapes, and society bombards us with glamorized addictions.

Our individual well-being from birth onward reflects the influence of a multitude of factors as psychology and biology interact. Three psychobiological factors normally contribute to the start of addictive behavior.

We experience a state of mind or body (usually negative) that we decide (consciously or unconsciously) to alter.

We discover a substance or behavior that "improves" that state of mind or body.

The consequences of this behavior commonly aren't immediately severe.

Drinking to Addiction

His physician referred Greg to alcohol treatment because his drinking had led to pancreatitis. Greg was unhappy and worried after moving to a new community and said he'd always had a hard time dealing with change. He also reported he'd felt depressed most of his life.

Greg described his father as an unhappy beer drinker who was bitter and withdrawn. He didn't spend the time with Greg that his son needed. Greg's mother was unhappy about her husband's passivity and dissatisfied with the family's finances. Greg's grandfathers on both sides were alcoholics. Because of negative childhood experiences around her father's drinking, his mother didn't drink at all.

Greg felt awkward with and intimidated by girls as a teenager, but felt confident when he drank. His humor and antics at parties gained acceptance from friends, and alcohol became a staple of his social life. In college Greg binged frequently and often passed out. After an arrest for drunk driving, he attempted to drink moderately, but failed as a social drinker. His doctor told him he'd have to stop drinking altogether because drinking was leading to severe health consequences.

Finding a Favorite Escape

During adolescent and early adult experimentation with different escapes, we often discover and "fall in love" with an escape or substance that offers dramatic and positive changes in consciousness. Favored escapes create biological/neurological interactions that we experience as "just right." Then, we learn we can suppress feelings of loneliness, anxiety, depression, inadequacy, or shame and feel euphoric instead. We describe our escape experiences in enthusiastic terms, such as, "I feel confident and powerful when I drink," "When I parachute, I feel really alive," or "Eating ice cream, I feel peaceful and content."

Adult escapes often flow from our satiation, arousal and fantasy childhood self-comforting strategies described by Milkman and Sunderwirth (Craving for Ecstasy). Using alcohol, taking tranquilizers, overeating, and spending are satiation behavior patterns. Cocaine, amphetamines, risk taking, gambling, cigarettes, and sexual seduction and masturbation are arousal behavior patterns. Marijuana, television, movies, and romantic novels are <u>fantasy behavior patterns</u>. During recovery, we must learn to replace our addictions one by one, stopping those causing the most damage first.

A Cycle of Eating, Purging, and Fantasy

Renee's father was in the army, and the family moved frequently while she was in grade school. She hated to leave her friends and try to fit into a new school and often felt fearful and lonely. Renee created a fantasy world where she was surrounded by people who loved her.

Her parents fought bitterly with each other when Renee was little, and she learned later her father had had many sexual affairs. With Renee, her father was distant and critical. Her mother was overweight, and when Renee felt insecure or discouraged, her mother often offered her baked goods to eat. Renee associated eating with security amid painful events. Her habit was taking snacks from the refrigerator and retreating to her room with her books and drawing.

As a teenager, Renee ate to comfort herself, but was ashamed of her weight gain. She spent her free time reading romantic novels and dreaming of a relationship with a perfect lover who would make her the envy of everyone. To avoid gaining weight, Renee induced vomiting to rid herself of food from her binges. By adulthood, she felt trapped in a secret cycle of distress, eating, fantasy, guilt, vomiting, and depression. Recovery for Renee began when she sought help to stop bingeing and purging. With support, she could face her underlying loneliness and pain.

Your Vulnerability to Addiction

Many people use potential escapes without becoming addicted—why not me? Addictions don't strike randomly—some of us are more vulnerable than others. You may drink to numb uncomfortable feelings like depression, anxiety, loneliness, social awkwardness, and daily stress, or you may use other mood-altering substances or behavior to distract you from unfinished feelings from childhood or earlier adulthood.

Unstable self-worth, unfinished feelings and PTSD, self-defeating life patterns, and family genetic risk factors all increase your vulnerability to addiction. The higher your risk, the more likely it is you could become addicted to alcohol, other mood-altering substances, overeating, gambling, sexual encounters, or other addiction. To overcome any kind of addiction, most of us benefit from general knowledge and information about recovery, as well as guidance specific to each addiction. Self-help groups for most behavioral and substance addictions are widely available. I describe addiction recovery resources and tools in Chapter 9.

Some people in recovery describe addictions as, "misguided spiritual yearning." This refers to feeling euphoric, peaceful, and connected to others when you're under the influence of a chemical or a behavioral addiction pattern, but these feelings fade away when you come down, and we often crash emotionally and/or physically to the exact opposite of the euphoric feelings we sought. The uncomfortable neuro-physiological truth is "for every high there is an equal and corresponding low." During recovery, we gradually learn how to feel content and connected to others without resorting to chemical or behavioral addiction.

Your genetic vulnerability to addiction may get triggered through the build-up of unfinished feelings, depression or anxiety, unstable self-worth, or traumatic life experiences. As research on addiction advances, we learn more about how each of these factors contributes to individual addiction risk. Estimating how vulnerable you are to addiction helps you make informed decisions during your recovery.

Recovery Exercise #14: Your Vulnerability to Addiction

Answer the following questions at two time periods in your life: (1) how things were (or are) for you at age 16, and if you're older than 16, (2) how they are for you now. Use a 0-10 scale where 10 means very true of you.

1. I don't respect myself.

2. Things from my past bother me.

3. It's hard to trust other people.

4. I don't take good care of myself with rest, diet, and exercise.

5. I get sick frequently or have pain and stress-related problems.

6. Depression, anxiety, anger, or insomnia are a problem for me.

7. Family conflicts bother me.

8. I have conflicts with friends, peers, employers, or co-workers.

9. It's hard to meet my responsibilities at home, work, or school.

10. I'm bothered by shame, guilt, regret or disappointment.

11. I've faced traumatic experiences in my life.

12. One or both of my parents were addicted to a substance or behavior.

13. I drank, used drugs, overate, or used other escapes at an early age.

14. I get in trouble, do self-destructive things, or make poor decisions around escapes.

15. There are addictions and/or emotional or mental health issues in my family tree.

Understanding Your Score

Possible scores on this scale range from 0 to 150. A score of 40 or less suggests that you have low vulnerability to addiction, scores of 50-80 suggest moderate vulnerability to addiction, scores of 80-120 suggest high vulnerability to addiction, and greater than 120 shows extreme vulnerability to addiction. Even if your overall vulnerability score is low, one or more high scores on the questionnaire could imply higher vulnerability.

Your total score at age 16 vs. your score now shows you how your risk may have increased or decreased. If you have high or extreme vulnerability to addiction now and are already addicted to a substance or behavior, it's unlikely that you'll be able to engage in **any** mood-altering substances or behavior without risking another addiction.

How Addictions Develop

There are four phases in the development of addiction:

Phase One: We discover an escape pattern we like. Once we learn about drinking alcohol, taking drugs, eating our favorite foods, having sex, going on spending sprees, taking physical risks, or other escape behavior, we frequently discover these actions feel good and don't have immediate unacceptable consequences. So, we turn to them again and again. We learn to rely on our addiction to achieve predictable changes of consciousness (Vernon Johnson, "I'll Quit Tomorrow"). As we become addicted, we have hundreds or sometimes thousands of experiences with these substances or behaviors, and rely on them psychologically and physically to cope with life. Although the consequences of our behavior patterns are often minimal initially, they often steadily accumulate.

Hooked on Running

Danielle was ashamed of her parents, who were both overweight. Her childhood resolve was to never become fat. As a freshman in high school, she joined the cross-country team and discovered she loved running. She continued running year-round and competed frequently in races and marathons.

Her husband was also an athlete and liked to stay in shape, but he didn't have Danielle's zeal. He felt she was overdoing it with her ten-mile daily runs, but it fascinated Danielle to push herself to her physical limits. She continued running even though she developed a chronic problem with one knee. If she missed a workout, she became extremely irritable.

A medical evaluation identified addictive exercising as a probable factor in Danielle not being able to conceive. Even though her running now seemed to hurt her health, Danielle found it extremely difficult to slow down. Running had become an addictive behavior pattern. Danielle had to let go of her quest for physical perfection to begin recovery.

Phase Two: Our problems and pain increase. On top of whatever problems we faced before we adopted our addiction, we create additional problems for ourselves in two ways: (1) we use a substance or escape behavior instead of taking action to solve our day-to-day problems; and (2) our addiction eventually leads to additional complications.

Flying High

Brent came home from school every day angry about a domineering coach. He couldn't stand up to this person, but when he smoked marijuana, it ceased to bother him. When he was stoned, school issues seemed less important, and he could relax and enjoy the evening. On weekends, Brent retreated to his hobby of riding his motorcycle. Risk taking became a way to affirm his independence.

Brent's anger increased until he felt ready to drop out of school. His parents worried about his marijuana use and were angry that he neglected his school work. When his mother criticized him, Brent would explode, venting his pent-up frustration about school on her.

Phase Three: We feel remorse over our actions. When we turn to an addiction over and over, our actions become self-defeating and inconsistent with our personal values. We erode our self-worth and create additional shame and regret, which leads to more escaping. Ultimately, we feel unable to stop our addictive behavior, even when we face significant consequences.

Shopping into Debt

To comfort herself about not having a boyfriend, Angela spent all her money buying clothes. Her parents had emphasized frugality, but Angela rebelled, telling herself that she needed to be stylish in order to compete professionally and socially. Over a two-year period, she spent all her savings. Even though she earned a good income, she was always broke. She resolved to stop spending money until she caught up—but the next time she felt depressed and lonely; she went on a shopping spree. Angela stopped using credit and asked a trusted friend to monitor her spending in order to start recovery.

Phase Four: Escaping becomes chronic. As time goes on, we prioritize escape behavior over personal values, health, relationships, and job responsibilities. Health problems, remorse, depression, or family conflicts often increase until we feel out of control and desperate.

Prisoner of Sex

Nick's father had extramarital affairs while Nick was growing up. When Nick learned of these as a teenager, he became very disillusioned. He felt outraged about his father's betrayal of his mother and resolved never to do that in his own marriage. However, Nick learned covertly that to be masculine was to be a ladies' man.

In college, he discovered he loved the challenge of making sexual conquests. He liked his reputation as a womanizer with his male friends. He saw himself as "sowing wild oats," but his relationships didn't last, and he would lose interest after the romantic phase of each affair. He began masturbating frequently while watching pornography.

When Nick contracted syphilis from a sexual encounter, it shocked him and it was humiliating to have to report to the health department. He recognized that sex had taken over his life. He didn't know how to have an enduring relationship, yet wanted marriage and a family. Nick's craving for sex had become a trap. He had to abstain from pornography and casual sexual encounters and learn to be intimate in other ways without the highs of a series of partners and pornography.

Image 8 portrays the crisis point in addiction, when accumulating problems threaten us with disaster. It portrays four addictions: alcohol abuse, cigarette abuse, food addiction, and addictive sexual behavior.

Last Supper at the Escape Café: Each cafe patron turns to his or her chosen escape for comfort, momentarily unaware of the looming disaster of genuine problems that will soon destroy this refuge.

Evaluating Your Use of Escapes

As a first step in recovery, identify which escapes (if any) have become addictive for you and don't serve your value system and best interests. The higher your addiction risk score, the more cautious you must be with any potentially addictive behavior. If you have a low addiction risk score, that's great, and means you have can devote your energy and time to other dimensions of recovery.

Destructive Escapes

Escapes that are illegal, involve physical risks, risk money you can't afford, or have high addictive potential are clearly dangerous. If you use street drugs, take part in other illicit activities, gamble or pay someone for sex, you risk legal and health consequences, humiliation, and lost self-respect. Binge-and-vomit eating cycles, excessive fasting or extreme diets, death-defying activities such as rock climbing without ropes or wingsuit flying, ignoring safety procedures in parachuting, kayaking, or scuba diving, dangerous driving; and driving under the influence of alcohol or drugs are all obviously hazardous. Some people can smoke cigarettes occasionally without apparent harm, but most of us who start smoking become addicted with all the accompanying health risks.

If you use destructive escapes, ponder the price you're paying and the risks you run. The following questionnaire helps you determine if a substance or behavior has become addictive for you. During recovery, you replace addictions, one by one, with positive, self-fulfilling behavior.

Recovery Exercise #15: Your Use of Escapes

Use a 0-10 scale for each statement about <u>each</u> escape behavior or substance use in your life, where 0 = very untrue of you, 4 = moderately untrue of you, 6 = slightly true of you, 8 = moderately true of you, and 10 = very true of you. Potential escapes include alcohol and/or drug use, food use, sexual behavior, exercising, spending, risk taking, gambling, or

_____.

My Use of Escapes

_____is a problem in my life.

I obsess about and look forward to _____.

I behave in ways I regret when I _____.

I _____to avoid negative feelings.

I attempt to change my _____and fail.

Your Scores

A score of 24 or more for a particular behavior pattern or a single item high score implies that you may have a problem with that escape pattern. If you have one or more addictive behavior patterns, you're not alone. Chapters 7 and 8 describe resources for recovery and how to develop your recovery plan. I present guidelines for replacing addictions in Chapter 9. Every step forward in recovery counts, so keep the faith!

Key Takeaways from this Chapter

- We learn specific ways to comfort ourselves as children, and these patterns may lead to adult addiction patterns.

- Many of us from troubled family systems are at higher risk of addiction because of the interaction of genetics, psychological pain, family patterning, and through discovering and falling in love with an addictive substance or behavior during adolescence.

- We often use a substance or behavior hundreds or thousands of times before we encounter severe consequences.

- If we're vulnerable to one addiction, we're likely vulnerable to other addictions, which we may mistakenly use as replacements.

- To begin recovery, we tackle substance and behavioral addictions first, because addictions often create so many additional problems that we're can't face underlying emotional and relationship issues.

9. A Wealth of Resources Supporting Recovery

"You're responsible for the effort and forces greater than you determine the outcome."

Anonymous

By making it this far, you've demonstrated your willingness to work toward the life you want and deserve. Accomplishing the remaining steps to recovery just requires your continuing effort, courage, time, and faith, in human proportions. If you act daily to improve yourself and your life, you can achieve a personal transformation, even though you control only your choices, not other people, places, or things.

Our past attempts to change our survival patterns usually failed because, unsupported and uninformed, we often became discouraged or overwhelmed as we confronted a lifetime accumulation of behavior, habits, and emotions. For many of us, our uninterrupted survival behavior patterns gradually or rapidly lead to disaster—unhappiness, illness, or complications from unresolved emotions and PTSD; self-defeating life patterns and addictions, or premature death from health complications, addiction, or despair.

Our survival behavior patterns were desperate solutions based on the extremely limited childhood choices available. Ideas such as, "I'll find a shortcut," "I can get away with it," "I'll win the lottery," "I can find someone to take care of me," or "I'll do it by myself" have got to go. We must realistically restructure attitudes, behavior, beliefs, and relationships during recovery, not suddenly or dramatically, but through day-by-day choices and growth. Our progress is sometimes so subtle we can't detect it. But gradually we sense the changes happening inside and ultimately recognize we've created different lives for ourselves.

Survival patterns are intricate, invisible, and powerful. By the time we recognize them and start recovery, we may have used these strategies thousands of times. It's quite a challenge to change such over-learned patterns, and we need specific knowledge, skills, and support with which to transform these behaviors into strengths. Fortunately, recovery information and resources are now readily available. This chapter describes central recovery tasks and explains how to use self-help groups and multi-dimensional psychotherapy as resources for recovery.

Recovery Tasks

You need to accomplish nine general tasks to accomplish during recovery. You don't have to do these in a certain order. You'll probably work on each task many times at deeper intellectual and emotional levels during recovery, but when you complete them, you can say, "I'm at peace with the past. I feel good about the person I am today and I'm excited about my future." Here are important recovery tasks.

1. Understand your life process.

2. Take responsibility for yourself.

3. Learn about and feel your emotions.

4. Heal from painful experiences.

5. Identify and replace self-defeating life patterns.

6. Discover and practice productive patterns.

7. Replace addictions with positive alternatives.

8. Plan for your future happiness.

9. Maintain your recovery.

Chapters 8-11 present guidelines about how to prepare for recovery and to design and carry out your recovery plan.

The following story illustrates Barbara's recovery from unstable self-worth and food addiction.

Barbara's Recovery

I'm 23 now and feel good about my life. I began recovery three years ago. I'd felt bad about myself ever since childhood. I'm the oldest child in my family and got a lot of attention and affection until I was three. Then my brother was born, and my parents, particularly my father, turned all their attention to him. I see now that this wounded me, and I decided there must be something wrong with me. I tried hard to get my father's approval by doing well in school and sports, but he still favored my brother.

By high school, I felt depressed. I dated a boy my freshman year and had my first sexual experience with him, even though I didn't feel completely ready. Shortly after that, he left me and started going out with one of my friends. I felt humiliated and angry and like I didn't belong anywhere. I started overeating after that and gained 40 pounds. I finally talked to my doctor because I felt so bad about myself. She recommended I see a therapist, which I did.

In therapy, I recognized my father somehow couldn't affirm me just because I was a girl. With my therapist's support, I've joined Food Addicts Anonymous. I've lost most of my extra weight and I'm following my food plan. I feel ready to date again, but I'll take my time about being sexual.

The Self-Help Revolution

Recovery information and self-help groups weren't widely available only a few years back. People trying to recover often sought help from professionals who didn't understand addictions and troubled family dynamics or used limited psychotherapy theories and techniques. As a result, many people floundered or failed as they tried to recover. Fortunately, all that has changed and now we have wonderful resources that dramatically improve our chances for success in recovery.

The self-help revolution began with Alcoholics Anonymous in the 1930s. Now, self-help information and support groups are available for most human problems on the Web, in community meetings, and in online meetings. If we struggle with addictive patterns like food addiction, alcoholism, sex addiction, or gambling, illnesses like cancer or heart disease, losses like divorce or the death of a child, or destructive behavior like child abuse or family violence, we can readily find guidance, hope, and support from others who have faced and overcome the same problems.

Self-help groups help us make sense of our experiences and gain hope. It's inspiring to see, hear, and learn from other people who've faced challenges like ours as they go through their own recoveries. We learn we're not bad people because of our problems. AA and other substance and behavioral addiction self-help groups show those of us trying to recover how the dynamics of addiction are more powerful than unaided individuals. This relieves the shame many of us feel about being "weak" or "immoral," feelings which can push us back to addiction.

Groups like Food Addicts Anonymous, Overeaters Anonymous, Sex Addicts Anonymous, and Gamblers Anonymous help members understand that addiction was a way of coping with feelings we didn't know how to face any other way. Al-Anon and Alateen help people who grew up in troubled families understand they're not "sick" or "crazy," but are experiencing normal reactions and adjustments to abnormal situations.

Many self-help groups follow the AA "Twelve Steps," which break recovery down into specific actions to accomplish daily. The foremost action in overcoming any addiction is not engaging in the addictive behavior for any reason. AA wisdom says, "If you don't want to get drunk, don't take the first drink, one day at a time," and Food Addicts Anonymous (FAA) says, "Don't take the first bite of any addictive food." The 12 steps guide people through six phases for recovery: (1) acknowledging and accepting the truth about our difficulties, (2) becoming willing to accept help from a power greater than ourselves which can be other recovering people or spiritual beliefs, (3) learning lessons from the past and acting to change ourselves for the better, (4) righting the harm we've done to ourselves and others to the best of our ability, and (5) developing a realistic and satisfying new way of life, (6) sharing our experience and understanding to help others who are seeking to overcome similar challenges.

Twelve-step groups are spiritual ways of living. They ask each person to define a "power greater than ourselves" as a resource for dealing with life. People's definitions of their "higher power" range from viewing the group as a higher power, trusting natural laws, accepting a traditional religion-based view of a higher power, or remaining atheist or agnostic while surrendering to clear guidelines for living without addiction.

Self-help groups stress taking responsibility for your own life and recovery, but you don't have to do it alone. You can ask for help from others, but you supply the elbow grease. Those of us who grew up in troubled families find acceptance, guidance, and encouragement in recovery support groups. You can find emotional support and choose to never be lonely again, so consider joining a self-help group as a resource during your recovery.

Recovery Oriented Psychotherapy

Sigmund Freud created the first formal psychological helping relationship with psychoanalysis, which emphasized the critical development importance of the first five years of life. Each psychological theory and technique developed since Freud has contributed to our understanding of how people and lives develop. A single approach, however, often doesn't sufficiently explain and help people change the complex survival behavior patterns used by children and adults from troubled families. Multi-dimensional psychotherapy integrates major discoveries from psychotherapy, family therapy, neuropsychology, cognitive psychology, and the study of addictions into the helping process.

Each of the following dimensions of change is essential to guide and support people recovering from unstable self-worth, problem emotional patterns and addictive behavior:

Opportunities for new relationship learning. The relationship between a psychotherapist and client is the foundation of helpful change. We need helpers who care about us and are warm and direct. We learn about successful relationships by solving any conflicts that arise between ourselves and our helpers. Psychotherapy provides a kind of "re-parenting" in which we receive undivided and compassionate attention. This is a healing alternative to our often difficult relationships with our parents.

Practice in compassionate self-understanding. As we understand ourselves and receive respect in psychotherapy, we learn to treat ourselves in new, strengthening ways. We understand ourselves more compassionately in terms of family limitations rather than through dehumanizing diagnostic terms like "neurosis" or "personality disorder," which many people feel imply being "sick," "weak," or "bad." Dr. Ken Burns describes how to change negative internal dialogue in which we discount ourselves, exaggerate events, jump to conclusions, personalize, or say harsh and degrading things to ourselves. We gradually recognize and change critical self-statements into realistic and supportive internal messages (Feeling Great: The Revolutionary New Treatment for Anxiety and Depression).

Direct problem solving and new skill development. Survival behavior patterns are often invisible to those of us caught up in them. We need logical explanations and direct feedback about what action to take. A person addicted to alcohol or some other substance needs to hear directly that alcohol or drug use threatens his or her health and safety (and often that of others), driving loved ones away, and that it would be in his or her best interest to stop drinking or drugging. But self-understanding alone doesn't lead to behavior change. We need support and careful teaching as we develop and practice new, more effective skills. To recover, an addicted person needs to learn ways to relax without their addiction, how to express painful feelings, and how to build genuine self-respect and self-worth.

Support in facing painful life experiences. Feelings of grief, anger, hurt, disappointment, and shame arise during recovery as we remember and recount painful events. We require safety and understanding to face these feelings and move on. Powerful emotions also accompany new realizations or decisions during recovery. For instance, we may recognize that we never felt safe as children, and experience grief about not having the chance to be carefree and innocent. As we give up addictions, we may feel anger and grief that escapes we relied on for solace or fun are no longer available.

Encouragement for self-responsibility and self-care. Our growth during recovery is directly proportional to the efforts we make. We need encouragement and guidance to take responsibility and instruction on specific tasks assists our learning process. We learn positive self-care skills, including nutrition, exercise, health care, recreation, relaxation, and spiritual self-development.

Two Trauma Resolution Approaches

Two specific psychotherapy approaches that I have direct experience with can effectively complement and support the integration and mastery of painful life events and traumatic experiences: Eye Movement Desensitization and Reprocessing (EMDR), and Multi-Modal Experiential Psychotherapy.

Eye Movement Desensitization and Reprocessing (EMDR)

Psychologist Francine Shapiro (https://amzn.to/3yCfxL3) discovered this approach when she observed that moving her eyes left and right several times reduced disturbing memories. She formalized this approach and established a worldwide network of therapists and researchers who have refined this technique (called bi-lateral stimulation and now including modalities beyond eye movements) to help millions of people reduce the negative effects of traumatic experiences. Many studies validate EMDR as effective for trauma reduction.

How EMDR Works

The positive impact of EMDR results from stimulating the left and right brain hemispheres in an alternating fashion through eye movements or using sound or vibration. These left and right stimuli appear to "wake up" targeted traumatic memories originally stored haphazardly in the brain. Properly applied, EMDR helps the person integrate memories in a more positive way, and gain an expanded perspective on very disturbing events, so negative affects like anxiety and anger decrease. As part of an overall recovery program, EMDR can help with depression, panic attacks, specific fears and phobias, childhood abuse and neglect, compulsive behavior patterns, nightmares, PTSD, and the symptoms of traumatic brain injury.

Multi-Modal Experiential Psychotherapy

Purely verbal psychotherapy approaches often prove insufficient for persons dealing with severe trauma. Multi-Modal Experiential Psychotherapy refers to a range of techniques originating with psychodrama, developed by Psychiatrist J.L. Moreno (The Essential Moreno). The essence of the experiential psychotherapy approach is that instead of "talking about" feelings, traumatic events or relationships, these feelings, events, and relationships are re-enacted in a group to facilitate deep emotional access and the expression of grief, anger, and other powerful emotions.

A person can thus tell his or her story in a way that facilitates both emotional resolution and behavior change. The process allows persons to receive support from others who have shared similar experiences and to accept nurturing and develop compassion for themselves. Experiential psychotherapy approaches are most effective for people who have stabilized their lives and established addiction recovery. Effective grief and trauma resolution reduces the probability of addiction relapse and can create a general improvement in health, vocational and social functioning.

Criteria for Participation in Experiential Psychotherapy

- The ability and commitment to refrain from self-destructive and violent behavior.
- Three months of continuous abstinence for persons recovering from alcoholism, chemical dependency, or from eating disorders or sexual addiction.
- Sufficient ego and personality strength to tolerate the emotional intensity of this type of work.

Considering Professional Help

Through this book, you've completed self-assessments of your well-being, including your basic human needs, your self-worth, your unresolved emotions, evaluating your addiction risk, and your use of escapes. If you experienced basic human need frustration as a child, grew up in a troubled family, struggle with self-defeating life patterns, are at high risk for addiction, or have developed one or more addiction, professional help can be a big asset to recovery.

If you've previously faced your challenges alone, consider giving yourself compassionate support. You don't have to be in deep trouble to benefit from the help of a professional, but certain symptoms suggest a definite need for professional help: (1) suicidal feelings or actions, (2) prolonged depression or anxiety, (3) violent or aggressive behavior, and (4) health complications. Use your best judgment in deciding when to seek help and what help is right for you.

James' Therapist Change

James felt he wasn't making progress with the therapist he had been seeing for two years. The therapist primarily listened to James with occasional comments. He felt more depressed than ever. He sensed the therapist didn't understand troubled families and provided little direction. When James joined a self-help group for adults from troubled families, and learned about survival behavior patterns, he recognized he needed a helper who had specific training and personal experience with recovery techniques and action.

You're Responsible

We may have the childhood illusion that we'll find someone to take care of us. The truth of adult life is other people will help us along the way, but won't carry us. If we surrender responsibility for ourselves, we're vulnerable to being victimized. The only exceptions to this are those moments in life when we're so weak, sick, or vulnerable that we must rely upon the compassion and good intentions of others. Most of the time, other people in our lives are there as consultants— and we pay the price if their advice is wrong. Our "consultants" want nothing bad to happen to us, but if it does, we're responsible. Find the best consultants you can, but make your own final decisions.

Image 9 illustrates this principle.

Fly by Your Own Instruments: Flying our small plane during a threatening storm represents the tough parts of our journey through life. Winds, thunderheads, and jagged peaks can destroy us in our fragile machine if we don't use all our wisdom and skill to maneuver our way through to clear skies on the other side. We consult by radio with advisors on how to proceed, but only by reading our own instruments, making our best judgments, and using all our skill do we ultimately get through. Please fly by your own instruments!

Your Commitment to Recovery

Personal recovery doesn't mean "as good as new." It means we can become happier, freer, wiser, more productive, more grateful, and humbler, even while carrying scars and memories of painful times and painful choices. Review in your mind all that you've been through so far. Remember the personal courage, determination, and toughness you've mustered to survive your challenges. And remember the people who have made a difference in your life by believing in you or by bestowing kindness. In recovery, you can achieve the deep satisfaction that comes from living according to your values. There are many people out there who can help and support you along the way. Make an unwavering decision to do everything in your power to move beyond your family trauma to a healthy and happy live.

Key Takeaways from this Chapter

- We now have a tremendous number of sources of information and help to support recovery.

- The self-help revolution has spread around the world, and now there are available support groups for almost every challenge human beings face.

- Self-help groups provide information, support, guidance, and myriad examples of people just like you who have faced and overcome the challenges of troubled families, childhood survival patterns that carry into adulthood, painful and traumatic life events, and addictions of all varieties.

- There have been enormous steps forward in the development and availability of psychotherapy and treatment approaches specific to people who grew up in troubled families and who suffer from enduring emotional adjustments, self-defeating life patterns and addictions.

- The foundation of your recovery is your decision—I'll go to any lengths to understand myself, change my life in the ways I need to, and discover the freedom to live without the burden of archaic survival patterns and their adult aftermath.

10. Getting in Shape for Recovery

"Thoughts become words, words become actions, actions become habits, and habits become destiny."

Patanjali, 11th Century Indian Mystic

You began your recovery when you sought information about changing your life. You've gathered additional information from this book and other sources. You may recognize yourself in the survival patterns described. Understanding and facing these powerful patterns is a big step forward and now is a perfect time to prepare to join the millions of people finding balanced and satisfying ways of life, free of family survival patterns and addictive behavior. You can achieve this freedom too!

Chapter 1 described the seven stages of behavior change: *recognition, hope, clarity, decision, preparation, action, and maintenance.* You've made progress with recognition, hope, clarity, and decision. Now it's time for preparation. As you prepare, you gather strength and resources to transform your lifelong survival patterns into a freedom lifestyle. Like training for a 10-K or marathon, you strive to improve your form and increase your stamina for the upcoming challenge. Begin your recovery conditioning using the recovery processes described in this chapter: "Caring for Your Inner Self" and "Designing a Personal Recovery Plan." When you have these started, you'll be ready to carry out the action tasks described in Chapters 10, 11, and 12, then maintenance in Chapter 13.

Caring for Your Inner Self

Eric Berne described our inner selves as having parent, adult, and child parts (Transactional Analysis in Psychotherapy). Our parent self includes our ability to make positive or negative judgments and choices. Our adult self includes knowledge, competence, and problem solving. Our child self encompasses emotions, intuition, creativity, humor, spontaneity, sexuality, and spirituality. During recovery, we expand beyond the limits of the survival selves we developed and broaden our perspective, develop new knowledge and skills, and connect to feelings, intuition, and creative potential.

Through this book, you've examined your life with additional information. You may recognize how your childhood family met certain needs, but didn't provide other crucial elements for your well-being. The deprived, hurt, rejected, ashamed, frightened, sad, angry, or lonely boy or girl of your childhood remains with you and his/her negative emotions and memories can block your positive possibilities. To heal you learn to "re-parent" your child-self during recovery (Healing the Child Within) as you do with any young children you care for. When you nurture and protect the little boy or girl within you, your child-self can provide energy, spontaneity, creativity, spirituality, and fun. These child qualities can gradually transform your life into a joyful and worthwhile experience. The following recovery tools help you nurture your inner child as you build strength and overcome unstable self-worth and painful memories.

Gentle Words for Yourself

Unfortunately, many of us speak to ourselves internally in the same harsh ways people spoke to us as children. This self-criticism perpetuates our childhood shame and unstable self-worth. Be aware of what you say to yourself during your recovery because your child self believes what you say, even if it's exaggerated or completely false. If we say degrading, critical, or frightening things to ourselves, we feel ashamed, inadequate, or scared. Therapists Mary and Robert Goulding say, *"If you tell yourself ghost stories, don't be surprised when you can't sleep at night."*

When you substitute forgiving, encouraging, and hopeful internal dialogue, your child self feels safe, lovable, competent, and brave. During recovery, practice interrupting your self-criticism and saying something compassionate to yourself instead such as, "I didn't know how to do it differently," "I'm learning through experience," or "I'm trying out new options as best as I can." Compassion words work. Reading a daily affirmation book you relate to can help.

Recovery Exercise #16: Your Self-Care Plan

What do you need to do regularly to feel happy, healthy, and calm? Set some self-care goals to work toward at your own pace. Don't expect yourself to accomplish these goals immediately or perfectly. These are objectives to orient toward and accomplish as you're able. List activities in each of the following areas you would like to do for yourself on a daily or weekly basis.

- **Physical health care** including diet; exercise; rest; massage and bodywork, and medical, dental, or other professional care

- **Emotional well-being** including contacting friends, self-help groups, workshops, journal writing, or psychotherapy

- **Spiritual well-being** including daily readings, yoga, meditation, prayer, church attendance, or communing with nature

- **Intimate relationships** daily or weekly time set aside for family members and close friends

- **Meaning and accomplishment** long-term goals and aims in your work and personal life that provide a sense of excitement and direction in your daily life

- **Recreation and fun** laughter, playing, being out in nature, and withdrawing from problem-solving activity

Reread your self-care plan regularly. Monitor your progress, but be forgiving if it takes longer than you expect. Most of us spend several years getting our self-care plan fully in place. Update your plan when you need to.

Recovery Exercise #17: Develop Your Recovery Plan

Successful projects start with a clear picture of the present situation and a vision of your goal. Write what you've learned about your survival patterns to give yourself the baseline against which to measure your progress. Then you can design exactly how you want things to be instead.

Below is a list of enduring emotional adjustments, self-defeating life patterns, addictions, and complications we've covered. Note each pattern and complication that applies to you in your recovery journal.

Examples of Survival Behavior Patterns and Complications

Enduring Emotional Adjustments	Self-Defeating Life Patterns	Addictions	Complications
Unstable Self-Worth	Compulsive Achievement	Alcohol or Substance Abuse	Neglecting Self-Care, Diet and Exercise
		Tobacco Addiction	
Unresolved Emotions and PTSD	Co-Dependency	Food Addiction	Health Problems
			Depression, Anxiety or Insomnia
		Bingeing or Vomiting	
Difficulty Trusting	Generalized Rebellion	Death Defying Activities	Painful feelings such as guilt, helplessness, anger or disappointment
	Casualty Syndrome	Compulsive Sexual Behavior	
			Family Conflict
		Compulsive Spending	Relationship Conflict
	Under-Responsibility Pattern	Compulsive Gambling	Work Conflict
			Burnout Symptoms such as cynicism, apathy or fatigue

For each issue, write a brief description of how that pattern appears in your life now. This is a snapshot of your "survival" pattern. Then describe the pattern of living you want to replace the old pattern, even if you don't know exactly how you'll accomplish this. This is a snapshot of your "freedom" pattern. An example recovery plan follows the list.

This exercise requires effort and thought and may take some time to complete, but your written personal plan is extremely important. Writing things down is a powerful tool for change, and once you have your plan, it's a helpful reminder of your recovery goals.

Zach's Recovery Plan

Zach became depressed after he lost his job as a sales rep. He worried about his career, his marriage, and his drinking. He identified four survival patterns he wished to replace with freedom patterns: (1) unstable self-worth, (2) unresolved emotions, (3) casualty syndrome, and (4) alcohol abuse.

1. Unstable Self-Worth "I feel like a failure because I just lost my job. I spend so much time down and doubting myself I can't get organized to look for work, and I have zero energy. I'm doing something seriously wrong in my life. I'm not contributing much to the world. I feel unworthy of my wife's love. It's like I'm getting away with something because she believes in me. When she realizes I'm a failure, I'm afraid she'll leave."

Goal: Stable Self-Esteem "I like where I am in my life, what I'm doing and that I'm an excellent partner. I trust myself and if something goes wrong, I know I've done my best and don't have to blame myself. I deserve to be with someone as special as my wife, and I accept her respect for me. I've found a satisfying job that lets me use my talents. I have energy and enthusiasm and I contribute to the world being decent, straightforward, and positive with people and meeting my responsibilities."

2. Unresolved Emotions "I've felt lonely and angry off and on ever since my parents divorced when I was twelve. I knew they weren't getting along, but I wanted them to stay together.

My mother kicked my dad out because he wasn't taking his share of responsibility for the family. He only worked occasionally, and she mostly supported us. I felt ashamed because in a small town everyone knew about it and gossiped about us.

"Before the divorce, my dad things with me like fishing and camping. Afterwards, he moved away, and I only saw him a few times a year. He felt I was on Mom's side because I decided I wanted to live with her. I haven't felt close to him since, and that hurts. I never talked about my feelings to either of them."

Goal: Feel at Peace with the Past "My parents' divorce paralyzed me as a kid because I felt abandoned by my dad and ashamed my family was falling apart. I'm not responsible for their choices. I realize their divorce had nothing to do with me. I've expressed my hurt about what happened and I'm ready to move on. I know what I went through is the same as other children from divorced families. I'll talk to my parents separately about what happened and see if it's possible to start new relationships with them."

3. Casualty Syndrome "I don't seem to know what's right for me. I thought my new job was what I wanted, but I lost it because my boss expected me to develop my market area more quickly than I realistically could. I knew from friends before I took the position that he was impossible to please, but I needed a job and was afraid nothing else would turn up. As I look back, I was naïve to think that it would work out."

Goal: Self-Responsibility "I know what kind of work situation is right for me. I don't do my best in critical and competitive environments. I'm learning what I need to do professionally and accept that I must learn certain things through experience. I trust my way of selling products, which is to build relationships with people who're interested in my product rather than hustling people who aren't ready or interested. I'll hold out for a position that's right for me, even though it sucks to be unemployed."

4. Alcohol Abuse "I drink a six-pack of beer after work and watch TV all evening. On weekends, I drink while doing chores in the morning and then have a beer open for the rest of the day. By late afternoon, I'm buzzed. My wife hates this because I don't feel like doing anything in the evening or I'm too drunk to go out. Sunday, I drink beer watching football and end up wasting the entire day and getting sloshed. By Monday morning I feel bad physically and worthless because I threw the weekend away when I could have accomplished things around the house."

Goal: Non-Drinking Lifestyle "I'm at risk of becoming an alcoholic. My grandfather was an alcoholic, and I probably have a genetic risk. I'll feel good about myself and my life without drinking. If I drink at all, I end up drunk. I want to join a health club and swim after work to get in shape. Then I'll be able to do something constructive in the evening like read, work in the garage, or spend time with my wife. On weekends, I know I can get a lot done. I'll finish fixing the motorcycle I'm rebuilding, and take road trips. I'll go out with my wife without being half drunk."

Like Zach, you can design a recovery plan for yourself. It'll serve you well! With your self-care plan and personal recovery plan in place, you're ready for the obstacle course. Image 10 portrays this moment.

Image 10 portrays this moment.

Ready for The Obstacle Course: With support, training, and conditioning, you're fully prepared to enter the recovery obstacle course. The course presents difficult terrain and natural hazards, but the satisfaction of achieving your goals justifies the risks. Go for it!

Key Takeaways from this Chapter

- The odds are against us if we take on our entrenched survival patterns without information, support, and guidance.

- With all these recovery resources, the task is still challenging but doable. As with any complex project, planning, preparation, training, and resources are the keys to your success.

- Because recovery is a marathon, not a sprint, your daily self-care plan steadily builds your strength, hope and support system and empowers you to face each new challenge.

- The process of behavior change provides a clear map of where you've been and exactly where you want to go.

- When we set recovery goals, we don't have to know exactly how we'll achieve these things, but take faith from the fact that millions of people just like us have recovered from similar challenges.

11. Transforming Your Life

"Don't let yesterday take up too much of today."

Will Rogers

What did we really want and need when we developed our childhood survival patterns? We usually needed things like stability, affection, self-worth, and support. You'll find constructive ways to provide these things to yourself during recovery, maybe for the first time. Be thankful you found even desperate ways of surviving your difficulties, but now through recovery you have many new options. This chapter describes how to overcome addiction. Chapter 12 describes how to replace self-defeating life patterns, and Chapter 13 covers how to overcome enduring emotional adjustments. Chapters 14 and 15 address maintaining your recovery and creating relationships that support recovery.

The Transformation Process

It helps to focus on one recovery priority at a time. Even though you're mindful of all your recovery goals simultaneously, it's usually necessary to confront addiction early in the process because addictions actively create additional problems and threaten self-worth, health, and safety. Once you have an addiction recovery plan in place (if needed), the next logical focus is changing self-defeating life patterns because these also can create significant complications.

As you make progress ending addiction and replacing your self-defeating life patterns, you develop the confidence and focus needed to overcome enduring emotional adjustments. Sometimes, however, it's necessary to deal with childhood feelings before you're able to replace an addiction or self-defeating life pattern. "Always fly by our own instruments," (with professional guidance and consultation if needed), deciding what makes sense for you at that moment. Your progress in one recovery area strengthens and prepares you for growth in another. If you're quite wounded, as I was, it takes some time to do all these things, but each step forward counts.

Replacing Addiction

We may say to ourselves, "I just want to feel good." Unfortunately, our desire to avoid reality through addictive escapes was leading instead to disaster. Many recovering people regard their years of pursuing addiction as an expression of "misguided yearning for fulfillment." Age-old wisdom suggests the correct path to happiness in four guidelines for daily living:

- Be thankful you are alive.
- Live your life the best way you can while being true to yourself.
- Take care of yourself and meet your responsibilities to those around you.

- Contribute to your community and the wider world using the abilities you have.

These guidelines outline the essence of a recovery lifestyle. Addictions directly threaten our ability to live by these principles, so we develop <u>personal addiction limits</u> to stop addiction from continuing to undermine our well-being

Personal Addiction Limits

<u>For most of us, recovery means stopping our addictive behavior for good</u>. We can't safely continue using substances or behavioral addictions to escape once we're caught in the addiction process. This is true for two reasons: (1) By the time a substance behavior pattern becomes addictive, we've exhausted its life-enhancement value; and (2) almost no one succeeds in re-establishing a moderate reliance upon a substance or behavior that has become addictive.

Therefore, alcohol or drug abusers find it necessary to abstain permanently from all mood-altering substances. People who addictively eat sugar, wheat, flour, and high-fat foods usually learn that their personal limit is to eat no foods in these categories under any circumstances. Addictive spenders may decide in recovery that they must buy nothing on credit. People who have become sex addicts recognize that recovery means being sexual only with a committed partner.

A classic diagnostic cue for addicted people is the hope they can return to "social drinking," eating high sugar baked goods or other addictive foods moderately, or illicit or addictive sexual behavior only occasionally. Almost always, the person discovers through painful experience that if the door to the addiction is still open, they'll go through it and find themselves in trouble again. Alcoholics Anonymous' classic wisdom states, "If you don't want to get drunk, don't take the first drink." This holds for all addictions. Once we start any addictive behavior, most people ultimately lose control.

Recovery Exercise #18: Your Addiction History

If you have become addicted to a substance or behavior, write a history of your experience with each substance or addictive behavior pattern that troubles you. (Use Zach's recovery plan for alcohol abuse in Chapter 9 as a model).

- Describe your experience with that escape behavior up to the present, beginning with your first memory of using that escape. How frequently have you used the escape (look at time periods of about three months)?

- What problems in your life result from your addiction? How does your addiction affect your moods? Did you do things that harmed your health, self-worth, finances, relationships, or job (be specific)?

- What are the costs and benefits of each addiction in your life now? Is it worth it?

- What personal addiction limits make sense for you?

Living Within Your Personal Limits

It's never convenient to experience the discomfort of facing life without your customary escape. Today is as good a day as any to face the world with full consciousness! Tackle addictions one at a time, starting with the substance or behavior pattern that is most troublesome. You can replace other addictions more easily once you've taken on "the big one." Replacing an addiction means deciding one by one not to act on your desires to escape. Cravings (psychological or physical) will pass within a short time if you do something else instead. Drink fruit juice, take a walk, call a friend, or go work out. Take care of yourself physically, mentally, and spiritually using your self-care plan.

Recovery programs teach "HALT," never get too hungry, angry, lonely, or tired. You are most vulnerable to relapse when you're in a weakened state. You can break destructive habit patterns by making fifty to one hundred pro-recovery decisions. You <u>can</u> live within your personal limits.

Desires to return to your addiction will come up in circumstances in which you relied upon those behavior patterns in the past. The wish for cake and ice cream at a birthday tantalizes a food addict. A problem drinker might envision "a cold beer on a scorching afternoon." A person with a sexual addiction might fantasize about a "one-night stand" with a new person they've just met.

Resisting the Urge to Use Cocaine

Clint stopped taking cocaine without great difficulty during his junior year. At the end of the year, he suddenly had a powerful urge to get high again with his former companions, a reward he'd used in the past for sticking to arduous tasks. He resisted this urge because his written addiction history showed his drug use was ruining his health. The power of the desire showed the power of his dependence on this chemical, and he decided he needed to join a self-help group.

Addictions provide the illusion of making things better. Recovery knowledge allows you to make alternative choices in situations where your choices were absent or invisible to you before. Absolute clarity about the truth of an addiction in your life is the best inoculation against the temptation to return to it. You need to develop stark mental images of your behavior choices to help keep your recovery priorities clear.

Image 11 portrays the knowledge vs. illusion choice for a problem drinker.

Look through the Bottom of the Glass: An attractive lounge beckons the drinker, promising relaxation, sophistication, companionship, and fun. The ultimate truth of the evening is humiliation, degradation, embarrassment, and sickness, as the drinker embraces his loyal friend, the toilet.

When you replace an addiction, you adopt a new identity that sets you apart from others. As you live within your limits, you notice many other people who don't—and they all seem to get away with it! Later, you observe those people who eat carefully and drink carefully or not at all, who don't smoke, and are loyal in their sexual relationships. You recognize looking forward to an addictive behavior, carrying it out, enduring the physical consequences, and feeling bad about yourself ate up a lot of time and energy. Breaking free from all that is a tremendous accomplishment. Your time and effort are now available to devote to things you couldn't get done before.

Without the anesthetic of addiction, you'll probably become more aware of the costs of your self-defeating life patterns and enduring emotional adjustments. You can now devote some of your extra energy and confidence to changing these survival patterns.

Key Takeaways from this Chapter

- The process of recovery takes place step-by-step. For some of us, like me, it took several years before I'd accomplished my recovery goals.

- Because active addictions threaten our health, safety, self-worth, relationships, and ability to make a living, often these are the logical first step in your recovery. If you need to, be sure to get professional guidance as you design and carry out your recovery plan.

- An essential beginning to recovery from any addiction is specifying the exact personal limits necessary for you to recovery. For most people, the only effective approach is to abstain from the substance or behavior which has become addictive completely. Painful experience teaches that if we engage in even a single episode of addictive behavior, we are at high risk of triggering the entire pattern.

- Once you have addiction recovery underway, you have the energy and focus to address self-defeating life patterns and enduring emotional adjustments effectively. Always remember, you don't have to do it alone. The wisdom, support, and example of other people show us the way.

- No matter how many steps there are in your recovery path, just focus on taking as many recovery steps as you're able today, and celebrate what you're doing. Every step counts.

12. Replacing Self-Defeating Life Patterns

"The only thing you have to change is everything."

Anonymous

Self-defeating life patterns originate with our childhood attempts to survive and meet our needs in troubled families. We needed recognition, affection, autonomy, attention, and accountability. If we become compulsive achievers, we probably needed parental recognition. Those of us with co-dependency often needed affection and security. When we became lightning rods and generalized rebels, we often needed respect for personal autonomy. Those of us who become casualties needed compassionate parental support and teaching. If we developed under-responsibility pattern, we may have needed accountability and encouragement to be responsible. You may have needed several of these forms of love.

Our childhood attempts to meet our needs could only partially succeed because we couldn't escape or change the family challenges described in Chapter 3. Our parents often couldn't parent constructively because they struggled with their own survival patterns and didn't have the information and resources to overcome them. But now we have all the information and resources to change our self-defeating life patterns—once we decide to do so.

How to Replace Self-Defeating Life Patterns

To replace your self-defeating life patterns, you must first recognize how these patterns play out in your life and how they work against your best interests. Then define recovery guidelines for each pattern which applies to you with revised beliefs and learned new skills to meet your needs.

Recognize Self-Defeating Patterns

Self-defeating life patterns are rarely effective at furthering our goals in our relationships and at work. We may have done our best in our childhood families, but other people didn't do what we hoped and expected. We then tried to get them to change them but couldn't. We bring these same expectations and sense of powerlessness to our adult relationships and work environments, and may unintentionally choose relationships and workplaces that don't meet our needs. In this way, we continually replay childhood themes.

Recovery Exercise #19: Your Personal Process Inventory

In your recovery journal, complete a "personal process inventory" examining the self-defeating life patterns you may use to clarify what needs drive these patterns and recognize where things went off the track. Before writing about your personal process, read through the inventory instructions and example below to understand how this works.

Inventory Instructions

Write about how you wanted things to be in (a) your family during childhood and adolescence, (b) in a significant romantic relationship or marriage (if applicable), and (c) one work situation.

What was your "job description" or expectation for yourself in each situation? Did you fulfill your job description?

What was your "job description" or expectation for the other central people in each situation? Did they meet these expectations?

If you didn't carry out your "job description" in a relationship or work situation, what happened then? Did you change your behavior, defend yourself, counterattack, try to conceal your failure, or leave the situation?

If other people didn't meet your expectations in a relationship or work situation, what happened then? Did you try to make them do what you expected by trying harder at your job, reasoning with them, complaining, withdrawing emotionally, being angry, or being self-destructive? Did they change?

What happened to your happiness, health, self-worth, use of addictions, satisfaction, and spirituality in each situation?

Brittany's Personal Process Inventory: Fighting for Her Needs

Brittany was a medical student who faced enduring emotional adjustments, co-dependency, generalized rebellion, and alcohol abuse during recovery.

In Her Family

"I wanted a happy family, parents who got along, a mother who didn't drink and was good to me, a father who respected me and spent time with me, no fighting, fun activities together, everyone loving each other. My job was to be a good kid, do my chores, do well in school, stay out of trouble, and be considerate. I did these things. My parents' jobs were to love each other, love us, enjoy spending time with the family, overcome depression, not drink, and get help if they needed it. They didn't do any of these things.

"To change things, I counseled my parents, supported them individually, confronted my mother's drinking, tried to get my father to treat her better, asked him to spend more time with me, pulled back from them, rebelled, got angry, started drinking. Nothing I did made things better.

"I ended up depressed and angry about my family. I'm ashamed of them and don't enjoy going home. I wish I didn't come from this family. I'm having a lot of emotional problems that go back to them."

With Her Boyfriend

"I want Jim to love me, affirm his commitment, plan our life together, share activities and accept me. My job is to care about him, do what I say I'm going to do, be loyal, be fun to be with, express affection, not over drink. I do these things; except he objects to any drinking. He doesn't want to date exclusively or be together every weekend, doesn't accept my drinking, and criticizes me and my family.

"I've tried to show Jim I'm a good person. I do things he wants to do. I'm kind to him. I've asked him to commit to me. I've slowed down my drinking. He doesn't want a long-term relationship, so I've pulled back. I feel insecure and angry and don't respect myself because I can't seem to just let go of him. The whole thing depresses me and I drink more even though he objects to it."

At Work

"At the clinic where I work, I want support for a research project I've proposed. I want a warm emotional climate for patients, and I want to move toward a more holistic model of patient care. My job is to deliver excellent patient care, continue learning, develop research ideas, and do my best to create a healing climate for patients. I do these things. The administration's job is to improve patient care, welcome new ideas from staff, support research, and support a healing climate. They don't do these things to the extent I think they should.

"I have pushed my research proposal, written memos, talked to administrators, argued in staff meetings, and distributed articles on holistic medicine. I haven't had the impact I want. Some people would like to see me leave. I'm labeled a troublemaker and I dread going to work."

Brittany failed to create the family relationships, romantic relationship, and work environment that she needed. Her efforts to change other people and systems led to more pain, which she suppressed with over-drinking. Her recovery challenge was to find successful ways to meet her needs for affection, recognition, and encouragement.

Developing Self-Defeating Life Pattern Recovery Guidelines

Exactly as you did in defining personal addiction limits in the last chapter (if applicable), define recovery guidelines to regulate each self-defeating life pattern that applies to you, revise the mistaken beliefs that perpetuate these patterns, and replace them with realistic information and experience and add new skills to balance your life. Here are examples of recovery guidelines, revised beliefs, and new skills for the five people whose lives illustrated the self-defeating life patterns in Chapter 6.

Justin's Compulsive Achievement Recovery Guidelines

I study, work, work out and plan for these activities only fifty hours per week.

I'm expanding my identity by developing additional dimensions of myself, including recreation, service to others, and friendships.

Every week I plan intimate time with family and friends.

I developed and am implementing my diet, exercise, and rest self-care plan.

I recognize and accept that academic and athletic success alone won't fulfill me.

I'm gradually learning to relax during unstructured time.

I practice expressing feelings and being intimate with others.

Justin's Recovery Process

Justin didn't seriously change his compulsive achievement until they'd been separated for several months. Initially, he enjoyed living alone because he could work to his heart's content, but soon felt empty and lonely, even after accomplishing a lot. Justin realized his open-ended achievements were progressively less fulfilling. He set an income goal to provide for a reasonable family lifestyle and decided he could achieve this by working fifty hours per week. This left him more free time to spend with his wife and children. He stopped smoking and reduced his drinking. He began getting in shape and rediscovered skiing and hiking, which he'd enjoyed before. He educated himself about relationships through self-help groups, reading, and workshops. When the couple ended the separation, he'd developed the skills to create new intimacy with his spouse.

Ashley's Co-Dependency Recovery Guidelines

I invest my time, energy, and affection in people who invest equally in me.

I honor my wishes, needs, and values in my relationships.

I take responsibility for only my part in what goes wrong in my relationships.

I let other people take responsibility for and worry about themselves.

I can't make anyone care about me, so if someone doesn't care about me, I look for a relationship with someone who reciprocates.

I pay attention to my feelings and needs in personal and school situations.

I'm learning to protect myself from unfair criticism or abuse.

Ashley's Recovery Process

Ashley recognized over the course of a year that her marriage would never provide a healthy environment for her. Her husband refused to see a marital counselor. Ashley was unwilling to continue with the financial insecurity and intermittent emotional attention he provided. After much preparation, she filed for divorce, entered graduate school in social work, and moved out on her own. She felt better about herself almost immediately. She took better care of her health and started losing weight. She felt more energy and enthusiasm than she had in years.

This initial high faded after a few months, however, and she periodically felt fearful and lonely. She began attending Codependents Anonymous (CODA) meetings and for the first time sought and found friends who were enthusiastic about her. With their support, she could face the financial changes and uncertainty of life on her own. After two years, Ashley met a man who gave her the warmth and respect she'd always craved.

Joseph's Generalized Rebellion Recovery Guidelines

I identify my personal and work responsibilities and do my best to meet them.

I don't have to be the "heavy" in most situations.

I'm not responsible for changing what's wrong with other people and organizations. I evaluate each situation according to whether my attempts to help will make things better or worse.

If I get angry about something, I use this as a warning that I may start a fight I'm powerless to win.

I focus my efforts on what I can change because there are many people and things I can't do anything about.

I try to let issues pass without challenge if they aren't really my business.

I'm finding people who support me in letting go of things that I can't change.

Joseph's Recovery Process

Joseph's preoccupation and anger about work finally led his wife to insist he get help. He started attending Adult Children from Alcoholic Families (ACOA) support groups. A friend there told him, "You don't have to save the world, just don't make things worse!" This shocked Joseph, but he recognized his continual campaigning had become destructive. He realized his reform movements began with his attempts to change his family as a child.

Joseph had to leave behind his resentment about his childhood. As he shared his hurt and anger about his troubled family and found that other people had been through similar experiences, he could stop struggling so hard to change his co-workers. He searched for a job with an organization he didn't feel compelled to reform.

Elizabeth's Casualty Syndrome Recovery Guidelines:

I clearly communicate my wants and needs to others in situations that affect my well-being.

I recognize I can't rely upon anyone to take care of me as an adult.

I don't expect other people to understand my feelings and needs unless I tell them directly.

Other people can advise me about how I live, but I make the final decisions.

I can't trust everyone and recognize and avoid people who aren't reliable.

I identify my feelings and needs in personal and professional situations.

I can protect myself from unfair criticism or abuse.

Elizabeth's Recovery Process

Elizabeth was in a financial trap with four children and few career skills. Feeling desperate, she entered psychotherapy at a reduced fee through a pastoral center. Elizabeth needed the encouragement and direction she'd missed as a child to solve her own problems. Through therapy and the support of her church, Elizabeth released the fantasy of finding someone to rescue her. It was scary to know she had to provide for herself. Elizabeth took assertiveness training and practiced standing up for herself with her children and other adults. She won a grant to complete training as a data processor. Over a two-year period, she learned she could manage her own life and build security and stability.

Jacob's Under-Responsibility Pattern Recovery Guidelines

I do what I say I'm going to do.

I take responsibility for myself.

I don't ask people to make allowances for me.

If someone gets angry at me, I'll look at whether I provoked this reaction through under-responsibility.

It hurts my self-worth if I feel I'm getting away with something.

I understand that life is a balance of effort and rest, and I achieve very little of value without hard work.

Jacob's Recovery Process

Jacob's wife started attending Co-Sex Addicts Anonymous (COSA), a self-help group for significant others of people with compulsive sexual behavior. After a few months, she informed Jacob she would end the marriage if he didn't end his affair and give her control over his business spending. Jacob accepted these conditions to save his marriage and business. He needed someone to hold him completely accountable. Because his wife could do this, both his marriage and business survived. Jacob recognized he couldn't afford to have people close to him let him get away with under-responsible behavior. He felt the beginnings of genuine self-worth as he accepted responsibility for his life.

Recovery Exercise #20: Your Recovery Guidelines

What guidelines, beliefs, and skills will guide your recovery from self-defeating life patterns? Write these down, apply them at your own pace, and adjust as you need to. As you reduce problems from self-defeating life patterns in your daily life, you're ready to take on the next phase of recovery.

Key Takeaways from this Chapter

- Because we've repeated self-defeating life patterns so many times over many years, it's challenging but possible to change these entrenched behaviors.

- As with each recovery step we take, clearly understanding how these patterns show up in our lives and what they cost us guides us as we replace them.

- For self-defeating life patterns, it's normal to make gradual behavior changes over time as we identify faulty beliefs and learn replacement behaviors.

- Writing and journaling are powerful tools that help us confront mistaken beliefs and strategies from childhood.

- Neutral allies such as other members of self-help groups provide examples of recovery and support for the changes we make.

13. Overcoming Enduring Emotional Adjustments

"It is by going down into the abyss that we recover the treasures of life. Where you stumble, there lies your treasure."

Joseph Campbell

There's still more to do in recovery because enduring emotional adjustments still detract from the quality of our lives. It's difficult to leave addictions behind and change self-defeating life patterns fully until we face and overcome the unresolved childhood emotions which underlie these behavior patterns. We normally tackle addictions and self-defeating life patterns first because we need to stop creating fresh problems to achieve the calmness, self-awareness and focus necessary to face painful feelings from the past. This chapter describes the emotional healing process during recovery and guides you in maintaining your hard-won recovery gains.

Developing Stable Self-Worth

Our self-worth stabilizes as we care for our inner self, stop addiction, and replace self-defeating life patterns. Recovery progress on these tasks translates readily into self-respect, because we're living a life in alignment with our deepest values. Rather than beginning each day with remorse, shame, or fear, we wake up feeling positive because we regret nothing we did yesterday and behaved in ways we feel good about. We don't attain 100 percent improvement, but acknowledge and celebrate our progress.

When you make your best effort, you can accept your personal rate of growth. Sometimes your progress may seem slower than someone else's, but this usually means you had more to overcome, or faced greater deprivation or trauma. Your recovery path is unique. To appreciate your progress, compare yourself to your own past. Review your recovery journal from time to time, and you'll see how you've grown.

As children, unstable self-worth was a way of defencing against hurt or disappointment by lowering our expectations. Now we no longer must prepare ourselves for the worst by putting ourselves down and feeling unworthy. Ironically, we discover our greatest trials can become sources of wisdom and strength when we see them through. Our new capacity to be who we are and honestly share the truth of our lives has a powerful effect on family members, friends, employers, and employees.

People respond to our compassionate honesty with trust, feel safe to confide in us, and we realize we have new personal experience and wisdom to share. We transition gradually from humiliation to humility. Humiliation is the person-destroying experience of unworthiness, failure, and shame.

Humility is an honest self-respect that incorporates the awareness we've made mistakes in life, learned from them, forgave ourselves, and moved on. We're fully human.

Healing Unresolved Emotions and PTSD

During recovery from family trauma and PTSD, we must face sometimes overwhelming childhood memories. To confront these feelings, we need the help, support, and guidance from people who know the way through. Powerful childhood feelings can often arise suddenly, such as when we encounter an authority figure who criticizes us, and we plunge into feeling profoundly ashamed, humiliated, and vulnerable from long-forgotten childhood moments. Being plunged into "childhood consciousness" can devastate us when we don't realize what's happening to us, and we momentarily lose access to our adult skills and awareness. In the past, experiences of childhood pain often drove us again and again back to addiction. It feels as if we can't survive such extreme distress, but keep in mind the recovery saying, "This too shall pass."

When we're hurt, a common instinct is to push other people away, but we can't heal well alone and in fact we need kindness and safety. Surrendering to vulnerable emotions like grief in the presence of loving and supportive people is transforming. When we take risks with safe people (in support groups, for example), we can receive the unconditional positive regard we yearned for, and experience tenderness, forgiveness, peace, love, and joy.

We learn, "it's impossible to look good and recover at the same time," and thankfully, we don't have to. Here are some difficult emotional states you may visit in recovery, but these are necessary markers on your path to freedom.

- I can't stop crying.

- I'm in a black hole.

- I'm swimming through molasses.

- I'm caught in quicksand.

But eventually we arrive at:

- I feel on top of the world.

- I'm grateful to be alive.

- I'm more compassionate because of what I've been through.

Real Feelings vs. Racket Feelings

In our families, we learned certain negative feelings were acceptable and others not. So Mary and Robert Goulding point out we practiced the kinds of negative feelings allowed at home ("Changing Lives through Redecision Therapy"). Because we overlearned these permissible forms of emotional expression, they became "racket," or sham feelings that we unwittingly used to manipulate others. Some families were "anger" families and others were "victim" families, or "guilt" families. Adult racket feelings often appear dramatic because we've practiced them, but they cover deeper vulnerability and alienate people who witness them. "Anger" people are good at blaming others, "victim" people are good at being wronged and helpless, and "guilt" people blame themselves and apologize all the time.

These racket feelings backfire in adult relationships. Frequently, "anger" people really feel hurt, ashamed, and afraid. When they express racket anger, other people pull away, and they feel more alone and hurt. "Victim" people often feel helpless and hurt, but when they play the victim, it turns people off, who may then mistreat them more. "Guilt" people often want acceptance and love, but when they express racket guilt, people reject them and consider them weak. Thus, racket feelings become just another ineffective childhood survival pattern.

Once we understand what our "racket programming" is, we practice expressing genuine feelings. We can recognize someone else's racket feelings because we see the drama but feel repelled rather than drawn to them. Group therapy is a powerful tool during recovery because people can compassionately point out to us when they sense racket emotions and help us discover the more vulnerable emotions that underlie these defenses.

Our recovery task, once we get beyond racket feelings, is sharing our story with genuine emotion with people who care. We can momentarily surrender to overwhelming childhood feelings in safe settings, cry our tears or express our anger, hurt, or shame while harming no one. This emotional release frees us to move on with our lives unencumbered by this childhood pain.

As we recover, we understand we got stuck along the path of normal development and have a hurt, frightened, or angry little boy or girl hiding behind our adult facade. We revisit painful events of childhood or earlier adulthood, recognize our discounted feelings, and bring those hurts and traumas to new, functional endings. This opens new behavioral and emotional freedom, and we look and feel like different people.

Facing Abandonment

In group therapy, Melissa asked for help with her angry feelings about a violent incident in her stepfamily when she was eight. She described the dramatic family scene, but members of the group were restless. Several people pointed out to Melissa that they weren't connecting to any genuine feeling. Melissa had unconsciously chosen to talk about something that seemed impressive, but had no emotional connection for her.

Melissa felt ashamed after this feedback, but it spurred her to remember a time after her mother died (when Melissa was three) when she lived with an aunt and uncle who resented her. She asked a woman from the group to role-play her mother for a few moments so she could say goodbye. The entire group cried as the abandoned little girl sobbed in her mother's arms. By the end of the evening, Melissa, who had appeared very young for her nineteen years, seemed older and radiated a new calm and confidence.

Re-Experiencing Traumatic Events

Earlier, I described multi-dimensional experiential psychotherapy and Eye Movement Desensitization and Reprocessing (EMDR) as two useful trauma resolution resources. One reason for some past recovery treatment failures was because purely verbal approaches were ineffective for people who've experienced traumatic events. Just talking about what happened didn't touch buried and frozen feelings.

After we establish a foundation of recovery, including stopping addiction, we can face traumatic memories from our past while retaining our adult power and the support of a loving group or the safety of individual psychotherapy using EMDR. In these specialized settings, we can experience exactly what it was like for us as children, release anger and sadness, comfort our terrified or abandoned child-selves, and rescue them forever from the scenes that haunt them.

Release of Hatred

As a boy, his mother badly beat Christopher. When he was older, he emotionally punished women he dated. He felt remorse after he rejected or said mean things to his girlfriends, but he hadn't been able to stop the pattern. In a psychodrama group, Christopher re-created the scene in which his mother lost control and beat him until he was unconscious after he broke a window in a neighbor's house.

When Christopher re-enacted being beaten in his group (harmlessly, of course), he remembered his terror and hatred. He released his terrible anger at his mother by beating on pillows, shouting, and crying until he spent his anger. Then Christopher held a fantasy conversation with his mother, who was now dead, and for the first time could see within her the overwhelmed little girl who was herself abused as a child. With his anger and hurt behind him, Christopher's heart softened and he could forgive her at last. In his later relationships, Christopher had to self-consciously practice loving behavior with women, but this past trauma no longer indirectly controlled his life.

Facing Grief

To arrive at forgiveness and love despite the events of the past, we must experience our losses and process our grief. William Worden describes four tasks of grief (Grief Counseling & Grief Therapy):

- To accept the reality of the loss

- To experience the pain of grief

- To adjust to an environment in which what we lose is missing

- To withdraw emotional energy and reinvest it elsewhere

These tasks apply specifically to grieving a death, but they also pertain to the grief we feel, whether other family members are living or dead, that our families weren't the way we needed them to be. We recognize the reality of our losses, seeing clearly and compassionately how things went right or wrong as we grew up. As we recognize what the costs have been to ourselves and to those we love, feelings of grief naturally arise. We recognize the tragedy and waste of lives that so often accompany traumatized families, including family members who couldn't overcome their addiction and other destructive patterns, and died or committed suicide. We'll always feel sadness over what could have been but never happened, but our regret doesn't sink us or prevent us from going on to happiness and fulfillment.

We adjust to our losses by adding into our lives people and resources who give us back some of what we missed. We naturally withdraw emotional energy from our childhood families and invest it in our love relationships, careers, friends, and our own children. If we become parents, we discover how easy it is to make mistakes when parenting, and our compassion for our parents increases. We become ready to forgive. There are certain prerequisites for forgiveness.

- Grieving the loss and recognizing both our pain and anger

- Taking responsibility for our own part (if any) in what happened

- Discovering that we can go on with our lives

- Recognizing the mitigating factors (if any) that explain other peoples' behavior

- Understanding that our own lack of forgiveness wounds us

- Realizing that we also need forgiveness

By the time we experience and understand these steps of grief and forgiveness, we arrive at gratitude. As our hurt and anger fade, we remember and appreciate the good things that happened. As we learn more about our parents' childhoods and lives, we usually see that they gave us more than they received. We can't help but love them. However wounded we were, we survived.

Beginning to Trust

We sometimes lived in perpetual states of fear and insecurity as children. Further childhood wounding might have placed us in emotionally impossible positions, so we behaved as we do when we're physically hurt—constantly aware of being wounded and moving carefully to avoid further pain or damage. Emotionally, as children, this often meant not letting anyone get too close and avoiding vulnerability because we feared rejection, or rejecting others at the first sign of conflict or difference to avoid abandonment. As we heal from hurts of the past, we become less preoccupied about avoiding future hurts. We regain the capacity to face painful losses that may lie ahead for us and regain our capacity to take risks.

As we progress in recovery, we gradually overcome our distrust of ourselves, others, and the world. We consciously decide to make ourselves vulnerable in therapy or support groups, recognizing that our efforts to solve our problems alone have failed. We discover there's a better way. As children, not trusting was a way of protecting ourselves from greater losses than we could sustain. Our conclusions that other family members and our environments were unpredictable or untrustworthy were unfortunately often accurate, but we are no longer trapped in this way.

During recovery, we sometimes fear we won't continue to grow and learn. We get spooked that things are going too well and our old defenses come into play. We're tempted to pull the roof in on ourselves to avoid the disappointment of some unexpected disaster. Our addiction may tempt us back, and we're tantalized by the possibility of throwing away the recovery gains we have achieved. These are times when we must continue those daily recovery activities we know we need and avoid potentially destructive choices by just doing nothing until we feel more centered. When life trials overtake us, we draw upon our carefully built up "spiritual bank account" to help us make sane choices.

Dealing with our Childhood Families

Many of us enter recovery before other members of our childhood family get help. Some family members never get involved in recovery, while all members of other families seek help, attend self-help groups, and take part in family therapy to heal together. There's seldom a perfect match of different family members' needs, feelings, and behavior. Our recovery may involve being emotionally and physically apart from families that don't understand or support our efforts. Parents and siblings often fear that family secrets are being shared in distorted and unfair accounts (which they may be). Recovering parents find it hard to watch their adult children still suffering from childhood wounds and floundering while the parents pursue recovery.

The ironic truth of recovery is that when we stop trying to change or influence other family members and focus on ourselves, they may start changing. This almost never happens on our timetables and often requires further growth and new tolerance from us. Only after we've achieved substantial recovery for ourselves can we seriously consider attempting to help the people we love, who remain trapped in their own self-defeating strategies.

It's almost always best to wait until someone asks for help. Acting too soon by trying to force family members to change then becomes a familiar and destructive replay of our old expectations of other family members. Neutral people are usually the most effective messengers who family members can listen to, and emotionally uninvolved professionals are a tremendous help if you attempt an intervention for another person.

We couldn't trust our own feelings as children because we didn't have knowledge and support, but now we have adult information and life coping skills. Self-help groups let us observe people like us who confront, struggle through, and overcome their life challenges.

Sometimes we feel grateful we don't have to walk in their shoes, but they show us it's possible to maintain recovery in the face of anything—death of a spouse, terminal illness, troubled children, divorce, death or illness of a child, bankruptcy, imprisonment, or unemployment. There's a recovery saying: *"I was always complaining about the ruts in the road until I realized the ruts are the road."* As we overcome our survival patterns, we find we can master setbacks in life that previously would have sapped our energy and joy.

Image 12 portrays this mastery.

Dancing through the Rattlesnakes This cowgirl is the master of her environment, gracefully skirting the rattlesnakes that surround her.

Key Takeaways from this Chapter

- Your foundation of recovery from addiction and self-defeating life patterns provides the stability, calm and focus you need to face powerful feelings from childhood experiences

- We restore self-worth gradually when we've stopped (or at least slow down) creating external problems for ourselves and behaving in ways we regret while taking positive actions at the rate we're able that leave us with new self-respect

- Fortunately, there are a multitude of self-help and recovery therapy resources to provide safe places to experience powerful emotions and release them without harming you or anyone else

- Carefully choose people as recovery allies who have themselves walked this path, and they can provide the guidance and safety required to connect with and restore your wounded child self

- Relationships with your childhood family naturally change as you access new resources and grow. Always focus on following your recovery path, which may require some apartness from family members who feel threatened by your choices or are unsupportive

14. Creating Relationships that Support Recovery

"The world is full of magic things, patiently waiting for our senses to grow sharper."

William Butler Yeats

Unlike a biological child who is under your care for approximately 18 years, the child within is your responsibility for life. In recovery, you're able to face new setbacks and hurts that come along in life, but as mentioned earlier, recovery doesn't mean "as good as new." For many of us, our inner children can't tolerate exposure to abuse, insanity, and deprivation. It's essential to use your adult power, discrimination, and information to find trustworthy people and environments that support you in becoming your fully functioning recovery self.

Image 13 portrays our capacity to use our adult power to protect our vulnerable child-selves from abuse or mistreatment.

Protect Your Inner Child A mother lion models how we need to protect and provide for our vulnerable and innocent child-selves. Her cub is under her watchful eye, and she is prepared to use teeth and claws to protect her offspring from any threat in the environment.

All relationships operate within explicit or implicit <u>contracts</u> about how things will be between us and other people. For instance, in romantic or marriage contracts, there is usually an agreement that both people will be sexually faithful.

Contracts allow us to meet our needs in relationship with childhood families, in our love relationships, and at work. You identified what you need in these settings during your personal process inventory in Chapter 10. Some of our needs are non-negotiable. For instance, exposure to abuse, insanity, or deprivation is non-negotiable because these circumstances threaten our safety, well-being, and recovery.

In the past, we sometimes made contracts based on illusions, and the result was disaster. Frequent illusions behind our contracts were, (1) Things will change for the better, (2) I can succeed where others have failed, (3) I can get used to it, (4) I can find a relationship or job situation where someone will take care of me, and (5) If I don't act on this opportunity, I'll never have another chance.

Considering adult reality, we revise these to: (1) I can change myself for the better, but other people won't reliably change because I want them to; (2) I can succeed where others have failed, if I have the resources and strength to act, and if my goal is not dependent upon the actions of others who don't share this aim; (3) I won't get used to it—I'll get sick of it. I'll never recover a tolerance for toxic things I've been over-exposed to as a child or earlier during adulthood; (4) If I choose to let someone take care of me, I'll become a victim when my needs diverge from those of the person or organization that's caring for me; and, (5) If I feel compelled to act on a certain opportunity, it's often a sign I'm overlooking some problem in myself or in the situation.

Your Entrance Exam

Develop your personal "entrance exam" to guide whom you choose for close personal or work relationships. Your entrance exam defines your non-negotiable contract requirements.

Recovery Exercise #21: Develop Your Entrance Exam

Based upon your experience with people and job situations, what are the non-negotiable requirements (as distinct from preferences) you require in personal or work relationships to maintain your health and well-being? List two separate categories: (a) characteristics that I must have and (b) characteristics that I can't stand.

Sample Entrance Exam Requirements

Entrance Exam Example	
Must Have	**Can't Stand**
➤ People who like and respect me	➤ People who aren't facing their addictions or survival behavior patterns
➤ Willingness to resolve conflicts fairly	
➤ Respect for people and a spiritual concern for life	➤ People who habitually mistreat others
➤ Honesty	➤ Ruthless ambition
➤ Reliability	➤ Covert hostility
➤ Ethical	➤ Sarcasm or putdowns

Use Your Entrance Exam

Once you have your entrance requirements, evaluate all the information available about people and job situations before you enter new contracts. People show you directly or indirectly what you can expect from them during the initial interactions, but you must use your eyes, ears, and intuition. As you evaluate a relationship or job situation, pay attention to what people say and don't say, what you learn about the history of the situation or person, and how you feel during and after the interaction.

Ask questions to get the information you need. Compare what you discover against your non-negotiable requirements and discuss questions and doubts with someone you trust. If your requirements are present, proceed with the next stage of commitment to the person or situation. Your entrance exam contains your implicit contract requirements. If what you require is missing, hold out for what you know you need, but be prepared to say goodbye respectfully if you can't achieve this.

If you're currently in a situation that doesn't meet your entrance requirements, you can't remain there too long without harming yourself. Do what is possible to negotiate for what you need, and if you can't achieve this, find a healthier situation for yourself. Even if you only decide to move on, you're empowered.

Give Yourself the Life You Want

When I was 25, a mentor asked me, "How many days do you have left?" The question surprised me then, because it seemed most of my life still stretched ahead. But ever since, his question has been valuable to contemplate. We don't know how many days we have left, but we know for sure it's a finite number. Through our recovery efforts, we've now gained new freedom to make positive choices, put the pain of the past behind us, see the world as it is, and break away from addiction. Our task for each of our remaining days is to treasure that day as if it were our last. In this way we build lives we enjoy and are proud of.

In your recovery journal, write your vision for a perfect day one year from now, five years from now, and fifteen years from now. Plan for what you need to do to prepare for those perfect days ahead.

Key Takeaways from this Chapter

- The image of the little boy or girl within you is a powerful tool as you plan each day

- Let that little person know what the day will hold and how you will take care of him or her

- Now you have all your adult power, discernment, and information to provide an environment of safety, intimacy, excitement, and challenge in which that inner self can thrive

- Even though your child self has healed from painful and sometimes traumatic childhood experiences, he/she will always be vulnerable to people and situations that are chaotic, unsafe, toxic, untrustworthy. Heed your intuitive senses about these threats

- Negotiate each personal or professional relationship bearing in mind your entrance exam requirements

15. Maintaining Your Recovery

"We must let go of the life we have planned, so as to accept the one that is waiting for us."

Joseph Campbell

Recovery goes on for life, but we don't always have to work so hard. A time comes when we realize we're living freer, happier, and more fulfilling lives. We recognize we've gone beyond the limits of our childhood environments and become masters of ourselves, excited about our future possibilities. We recognize that our distress and that life challenges pushed us to grow, change, and learn. Many people in recovery describe how grateful they about how their lives developed because without suffering they would never have discovered and taken advantage of all the resources of recovery.

Facing the Ups and Downs of Life

Life will continue to present challenges, so in this chapter I introduce two coping tools—your instrument panel and the well-being checklist—to help you and your partner identify and solve problems and maintain your strength and spirits, no matter what. The next two exercises can serve you throughout life to make it through whatever challenges you face.

Action Step #22: Monitor Your Instrument Panel

Your Instrument Panel	
Enthusiastic Optimistic Energetic Directed Efficient	Green
Frustrated Anxious Discouraged Inefficient Worried	Yellow
Neglecting Yourself Compulsive Behaviors Conflicts with Others Fatigued Angry	Orange
Depressed/Anxious Insomnia Burned out/Exhausted Getting Sick Frequently Overwhelmed/Unproductive	Red
Serious Illness Thoughts of Suicide Drug and Alcohol Abuse/Addiction Severe Depression Despair	Black

Irritability is a frequent instrument panel warning signal for many of us, so if you feel irritable, ask yourself if you're tired, lonely, hungry, angry, stressed, or worried? If your instrument panel lights up, use the well-being checklist below to identify what's bothering you and develop a plan to get back on track. What's your instrument panel telling you?

Action Step #23: Use the Well-Being Checklist

When you get warning signals on your instrument panel, use the following well-being checklist to identify how to restore emotional and physical balance.

Be compassionate with yourself. Watch out for negative self-talk. Negative thoughts lead to negative feelings, which lead to negative behavior. When you're unhappy, first ask yourself, Am I saying negative things to myself? If you're constantly criticizing yourself and predicting the worst outcome for every situation, you'll walk around feeling ashamed, inadequate, and scared. Get a book of daily affirmations at your local bookstore and read it every day— these really help. Also, practice being compassionate with yourself by writing compassionate messages in your relationship journal.

- "I didn't know how to do it differently."

- "I'm learning through experience."

- "I'm taking action to solve the problem."

- "I've done my best and trust things will work out."

Write three ways you criticize yourself and three kind things you can say to yourself instead.

Correct your mistakes. Did you hurt someone or let them down—by being insensitive, irritable, or selfish, not following through, or not meeting your responsibility? These actions weigh on you until you take responsibility, apologize when you need to, and change your behavior. Are there any mistakes you need to correct? How and when will you do it?

Follow a daily self-care plan. Move forward with daily self-care goals at your own pace. You don't have to accomplish these goals perfectly—just aim for "progress, not perfection." List your daily/weekly self-care actions for each area below in your relationship journal.

- Physical health (diet, exercise, rest, and medical, dental, or other professional care).

- Emotional well-being (friendships, support groups, workshops, journal writing, or therapy).

- Spiritual well-being (reading, meditation, spiritual practices, retreats, or spending time in nature).

- Close relationships (time set aside for family members and close friends).

- Meaning and accomplishment (performing long-term work and achieving goals that provide excitement and purpose).

- Recreation and fun (laughter, playing, being in nature, sports, games, and entertainment).

Move away from toxic influences. Keep away from toxic people, negative environments, destructive media, and situations that bring you down. If you can't get out of a bad job situation right away, plan to leave the situation, even if all you can do is start the change. When you decide to act, you feel better right away because you've empowered yourself. What action do you need to take to move away from toxic influences?

Be grateful. No matter what problems you encounter, usually, some things are going *right*—you have a job, a caring partnership, your health, a place to live, or you can appreciate the beauty in life, art, literature, and nature. Remember the good things to keep your dark days in perspective. Life itself is a wonderful gift. List what you're grateful for and use it to remind you when things get tough.

Design a positive future. Short- and long-term goals support you in navigating life's drudgery and challenges. Plan something fun to reward yourself for what you accomplish each day and give yourself larger rewards occasionally. Have a plan for the important things you want to accomplish during life and partnership, and the next steps you'll take to accomplish each of these.

Serve others. As you learn and grow in your partnership, you have more to share with others. Any kind of volunteer work helps because you:

- feel the satisfaction of helping someone

- remember that you're part of a larger whole

- forget about your problems

- get your life back in perspective, and

- see the positive impact of your actions on others

What service can you provide?

Daily Recovery Practices

The last stage in the process of behavior change is maintenance—actions that maintain and enhance all the efforts you've made. These daily habits are common sense orienting points to help you get through each day without extra hardship (or the risk of going back to addictions or other survival patterns). These habits help a lot, and you can always add more daily practices to help you focus on the big picture—being the best person you can and not taking unnecessary detours. Below are a few suggestions.

Start and end the day with quiet time. Take a few minutes in the morning to check in with yourself and plan your day and be grateful to be alive. Think about challenges you'll face today and visualize yourself handling them smoothly. Read and contemplate something inspiring from a book of quotations or prayers, a spiritual book, or daily affirmation. Late in the day, review how things went and write anything you need to do tomorrow. Give thanks for the good people and things in your life.

Remain teachable. A friend in recovery mentions this saying often. It's a perfect reminder that we don't know everything. Sometimes we're just plain wrong or kidding ourselves, and we all have blind spots. When we learn something we didn't plan on, it helps keep us humble.

"How important is it?" When we react to other peoples' unacceptable behavior, like aggressive drivers on the highway, or people who act like they're better than us, we're at risk of creating additional problems. We're most likely to let other people's actions provoke us when we're out of balance. Recovery wisdom says, "Let the tailgaters pass."

"Seek progress, not perfection." We accomplish big things by doing our best one day at a time. Give yourself credit for the good things you do today. If you make a mistake, be compassionate with yourself, learn from it and plan how to make things better.

"Take responsibility." It's tempting to make excuses and blame someone or something else for our problems and mistakes. We all do it! Other people will do things that hurt and disappoint us but, when we look closely, we recognize we often had some part in creating our difficulties. Focus on your choices and actions rather than what others do. Most of us have plenty to do to stay on track. Improving yourself keeps you busy, so you don't have to meddle in other people's affairs.

"Surrender to Win." Focus on what you can control (your choices and behavior) as suggested by the Serenity Contemplation: "Grant me the serenity to accept the things I cannot change, the courage to change the things I can, and the wisdom to know the difference."

Tolerate uncertainty. A common anxiety we all face is wondering if everything will work out. When we're afraid, we're often tempted to force a solution. This usually prolongs the situation, or because our timing isn't right, makes things much worse. Being patient and doing nothing is sometimes the best (but hardest) choice.

Endure discomfort. When we hurt someone and apologize, we may want them to forgive us right away. However, they're still hurt and aren't ready to forgive and trust immediately. If we give them time and space to heal, people will often become ready to be close and trust again. If they don't, do what you can to make things right and let them go in peace.

Trust the process. Even though you do your best using all your resources to cope with change, you'll still encounter losses, tragedies, and setbacks along the way. Grief is a universal part of being human when people we love get sick, get injured in accidents, or pass away. With all your recovery resources, you can endure the grief process, doing your best to maintain your balanced life choices and accept the support of others.

Remember the truths of your recovery. While some people can enjoy potentially addictive substances and behavior responsibly, you may not one of those people. If you're vulnerable to addiction, this applies to all addictive substances and behavioral addictions. You need help and support to maintain your recovery. You're human and will make mistakes and can forgive yourself for your mistakes because you're genuinely working to create an alternative way of living. It's not your job to straighten out other people.

A New Destiny in Recovery

When we brought our childhood survival patterns into our adult lives, we unwittingly created further unhappiness and additional problems. This pain and distress ultimately compelled us to seek additional information and support. As we understand and replace these patterns, a new world opens. Our vision about who we truly are and what life is right for us may change during recovery.

When we reached out for help, we received answers and support that allowed us to overcome our challenges. These same principles apply to everything in life. Life in recovery is still challenging, but we can face each challenge as it comes, clear-headed and fully resourced. You are part of the vast community of people finding life beyond family trauma. I earnestly hope this book has supported you as you overcome your challenges and develop the life you want and deserve.

Best wishes always on your recovery journey!

Please Review this Book if you Would

If the book has been helpful to you, please take a few moments to submit an honest review on Amazon. This helps other readers decide if the book is right for them.

Sign in to Amazon then go to <u>My Orders</u>, select this book and it will offer you a link to write a review.

Thank you very much!

My Next Book

The next book in my Fundamental Living Solutions series is called *Smart Happy Love: Ten Practical Dating Guidelines for Meeting Your Relationship Goals and Creating a Lifelong Partnership.*

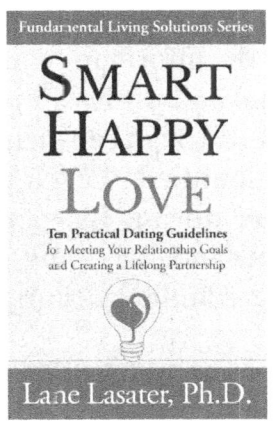

It was released in Fall 2021.

About the Author

Dr. Lane Lasater worked for 45 years in community mental health centers, corrections, schools, and in practice as a clinical psychologist, empowering individuals, couples, and families to heal themselves and forge satisfying life paths. Throughout his career, Dr. Lasater has specialized in guiding people who face common but challenging problems in living, including  overcoming trauma and addiction, creating healthy relationships, coping with family challenges, and raising responsible children.

Lane's focus is sharing the information and knowledge he has gained through personal and professional experience with as many people as possible through self-help books, audiobooks, and webinars. Lane identified the family trauma patterns presented in this book during his personal recovery and through work with thousands of young people and adults to overcome past challenges and take charge of their lives.

To provide practical life information for students from challenging backgrounds, Lane co-developed classroom curricula for youth and their parents that reached 50,000 young people and families in 17 states (bit.ly/3cs8dIB). For this work, he received a National Innovative Practice Award in Psychology from the American Psychological Association.

Lane and his life partner Nancy now live in North Carolina and enjoy hiking and kayaking.

Acknowledgements

This book would not have been possible without the great faith, patience, encouragement, and constructive criticism of my wife and life partner, Nancy B. Larson Lasater. I want to thank my sons who continually reminded me of the preciousness and importance of childhood. I thank Dr. Peter Ossorio for his friendship and inspiration throughout my career, for teaching me the principles of Descriptive Psychology, helping me conceptualize the book, and originating the use of images in psychotherapy. I thank all my teachers, mentors, colleagues, and clients who provided me with the joy and privilege of learning how to live in recovery and how to be helpful to others. I thank Janet Gustafson for bringing the images for recovery to life so beautifully. It was a joy to work with her. I thank 100 Covers for their creative cover design and great covers. 100covers.com

Certain people made significant contributions to my original book along the way: Laurie Lasater and Annette Nixon Lasater encouraged me to make the book straightforward and accessible; Bob Wells served as a valuable critic, keeping his standards high and connecting me with resources along the way; Dan Mason urged me to put myself into the book and made helpful editorial changes; and Leslie Burger did a beautiful job of editing as the book neared completion. Cecelia Maxwell suggested the Dream/Her Dream image, and Sophie Morgan suggested the Dancing through the Rattlesnakes image. Dr. Carolyn Zeiger, Shelley Stuart-Bullock, and Linda Reed suggested important improvements on the images. I thank you all.

Made in the USA
Las Vegas, NV
04 September 2023

77064217R00105